Table of Contents

Overview of the ASSIST Program

Affective/**S**ocial **S**kills: Instructional **S**trategies and **T**echniques

The ASSIST Program is designed to increase students' growth in self-esteem, self-management, interpersonal relationships, conflict resolution, and emotional understanding. ASSIST manuals provide a complete guide for elementary school teachers and counselors to actively involve students in developing critical personal/social skills. The ASSIST Program can be used as a K-6 developmental school guidance curriculum by following the scope and sequence at the end of this manual. It can be integrated into regular academic programs, or each manual can stand alone as a curriculum for personal growth or social competence.

The ASSIST curriculum is the result of an extensive review of child development theory and research, a review of existing social/emotional education programs, and the feedback of many teachers and students who participated in the program. ASSIST incorporates concepts and procedures from social learning theory, child psychology, and proven educational practices.

Each field-tested lesson includes:

- A "To the Teacher" section which provides a theoretical background for lesson concepts;
- A "scripted" lesson that provides the dialogue, examples, and practice necessary to teach lesson concepts and skills;
- A series of transparency masters which make lesson concepts accessible to picture-smart students;
- A series of reproducible worksheets which provide opportunities for students to process the lessons; and
- Several "Supplementary Activities" following each lesson which are designed to encourage the transfer of training.

ASSIST was developed with Title IV-C Innovative Education Funds and was evaluated in elementary school classrooms in four school districts. **Statistically significant gains in self-concept and social skills occurred in eight out of nine assessments.** As a result, ASSIST was validated in Washington State and designated cost-effective and exportable. It is now in the state's "Bank of Proven Practices," a clearinghouse for quality programs.

The ASSIST manuals currently in print include the following:

- ***Building Self-Esteem in the Classroom***—Both the *Primary Version* and the *Intermediate Version* contain all new lessons and activities. Students refine their self-descriptions and acquire an appreciation for their uniqueness. They learn that they are multi-faceted and that there are at least seven different ways they can be smart. They learn the cognitive skill of self-encouragement, which enables them to respond to mistakes, failures, or put-downs in a manner which maintains their self-esteem. They learn to take responsibility for their school success by using self-statements to motivate and coach themselves through academic tasks. A unit written for advanced or middle school students is also included in the *Intermediate Version*. (*Primary Version*, 926 pages; *Intermediate Version*, 670 pages)

- **Creating A Caring Classroom**—This manual includes a collection of strategies designed to promote mutual support and strengthen connections in the classroom. Included are: (1) getting-acquainted activities; (2) classroom management procedures; (3) a personal/social behavior scale and behavior improvement strategies for students with special needs; (4) a relaxation training program; and (5) a large collection of activities for establishing a nurturing classroom community. (400 pages)
- **Helping Kids Find Their Strengths**—This manual is designed to enable students to identify and utilize their strengths. It is based on the combined expertise of the theorists, researchers, and practitioners who worked on the Dependable Strengths Project Team at the University of Washington. Students are able to build their self-esteem not just by positive thinking but by analyzing experiences they're proud of for clues regarding their core strengths. Students share their good experiences, then utilize teacher and peer input to "tease out" the strengths that helped them create those experiences. They learn a large strength vocabulary and are able to prove to themselves and others that they have strengths they can depend on. They use their expanded self-identity as a springboard for new successes. In helping one another find their strengths, students develop a respect for diversity. (713 pages)
- **Helping Kids Handle Anger**—This manual includes lessons designed to enable students to acknowledge, accept, and constructively express anger. Students learn: (1) to use inner speech to inhibit aggressive behaviors; (2) to use thinking skills for choosing constructive behaviors when angry; (3) appropriate language for expressing anger; (4) a variety of techniques for releasing energy after anger arousal; (5) ways to defuse the anger of others; and (6) a model for resolving classroom conflicts. Role-plays and puppets are utilized to encourage active student involvement. (516 pages)
- **Helping Kids Handle Put-Downs**—This manual teaches students a repertoire of assertive responses to teasing that avoid reinforcing antagonizers. Students learn: the art of ignoring; surprising aggressors by "agreeing" with them; disarming aggressors with humor; and deflecting aggression with "crazy compliments." These strategies win respect and de-escalate conflict. Students also learn to use self-encouragement to dispel the hurt of put-downs and maintain their self-respect. (290 pages)
- **Multiple Intelligences: Helping Kids Discover the Many Ways They're Smart**—The purpose of this manual is to help students understand that they are intellectually multi-faceted. They are introduced to a process to assess their own strong intelligences. Students learn that each intelligence is as valuable as any other and gain respect for their own particular strengths, as well as those of others. The lessons in this manual are an expanded version of a unit on multiple intelligence in Building Self-Esteem in the Classroom. Additionally, this new manual contains a section of activities linking multiple intelligences with career choices. (333 pages)
- **Teaching Cooperation Skills**—This manual includes a series of lessons and experiential activities designed to teach students the skills necessary for cooperative learning to take place. Lessons focus on the skills of self-management, listening, collaborative problem solving, and leadership. Students learn to resolve conflicts through negotiation and compromise. Included are 52 activities designed to provide practice of cooperation skills and 55 cooperative academic activities in the major subject areas. (437 pages)

- ***Teaching Friendship Skills***—Both the *Primary Version* and the *Intermediate Version* contain all new lessons and supplementary activities for each grade level. Students identify the behaviors in others which attract them and behaviors which alienate them. They examine their own behavior and determine changes they need to make in order to gain friends. They learn how to curb physical and verbal aggression. They discover that the secret to making friends is to make others feel special, and they practice specific ways to do so. They learn the value of sharing and how to give sincere compliments and apologies. In addition, the *Intermediate Version* focuses on listening, understanding others' perspectives and feelings, and being honest but kind. It also contains 56 activities designed for a "Friendship Center." Each version provides a comprehensive bibliography of children's books on friendship. Puppets, games, role-plays, kinesthetic activities, and goal-setting are used to increase motivation and the transfer of training. (*Primary Version*, 537 pages; *Intermediate Version*, 605 pages)

Introduction

One of the major ways children's self-esteem can be diminished is through the teasing and put-downs of their classmates. There's hardly a child who isn't vulnerable to the critical comment of a peer.

In this manual students learn to handle put-downs by utilizing a variety of techniques, including ignoring the put-down, using their imagination to deflect the put-down, "agreeing" with the put-down, and use of humor. Through these techniques, students are able to disarm the antagonizer and deflect aggression. Their responses are assertive rather than aggressive. A number of the techniques involve responding to put-downs with playful retorts. By giving such responses instead of responding with anger and another put-down, students are often able to win the respect of both the put-downer and others.

When students are confronted with disparaging statements or insults, it's almost an instinctive reaction for many of them to respond in a defensive or an aggressive manner. Most also silently agree with the abuser and feel badly about themselves. In these lessons students learn that they can do something to prevent both of these nonproductive responses from happening. They can use self-statements that are both true and encouraging. Realistic self-encouragement can help students to not dwell on hurtful comments and can sustain their self-esteem at particularly vulnerable moments.

By learning to handle put-downs with equanimity, students who are the targets of verbal abuse are able to keep teasing and name-calling from eroding their self-esteem. They can also be spared some of the hurt that put-downs cause. Equally important, when students utilize the strategies suggested in this manual they can defuse and disengage from potentially violent interactions.

How to Use This Curriculum

Lesson Grade Levels

Each lesson in this curriculum presents one or more concepts that are central to building positive self-esteem. Because of the timelessness and generality of most of these concepts, the same lessons can be taught to students as they advance through the primary grades or through the intermediate grades. With each subsequent exposure to the concepts in a lesson, students are able to consider the concepts from a new frame of reference and make new and more precise applications.

"To the Teacher" Section

Each lesson has a clearly stated objective, a list of all the materials needed to teach the lesson, and a "To the Teacher" section. This section outlines the planning necessary for the lesson and provides theoretical background on the concepts presented. It also includes a summary of the skills taught in the lesson, the methods used, and suggestions for effective teaching.

"Lesson Presentation" Section

The "Lesson Presentation" section provided with each lesson gives step-by-step instructions on how to present the material. To facilitate the use of teaching techniques in effective education, scripts are provided in boldface type. These scripts are not intended to be used verbatim; rather, they are models of effective teacher comment and interaction. You will want to rephrase the scripts, saying things in your own words to accommodate aspects of your particular students' frames of reference. The success of the lessons will depend on your ability to provide examples and illustrations of lesson concepts that your students will relate to. It will also depend on your sense of how to pace each lesson, expanding or shortening sections to fit your students' needs. You should feel free to spend additional time on a lesson that seems of particular interest to your students.

Names are used throughout the lessons to depict fictitious children. We recommend substituting other names if there is any chance of embarrassment to your students. You may also wish to change names in order to focus positive attention on students of various ethnic origins.

As mentioned, lessons should be tailored to the needs of your students. To do so, you will need to be very familiar with each lesson before you teach it. One way to gain this familiarity is by taping a lesson and listening to it as you travel to and from school. You may also order tapes of these lessons from the publisher of this manual. Becoming familiar with lesson format in this way will enable you to ad-lib the lesson, freeing you to more easily handle the many transparencies.

Each lesson concludes with a debriefing section and techniques that facilitate generalization and the transfer of training to real-life situations.

Transparencies

Each lesson includes a series of transparency masters for picture-smart students whose learning style is "Don't just tell me—show me!" You may wish to color the transparencies with permanent markers. Using the markers on the back of the transparencies works best.

Handouts

Reproducible student handouts/worksheets also accompany each lesson. These worksheets give students an opportunity to process lesson concepts as well as to demonstrate that they were "attending and receiving" during the lesson presentation and discussion.

Supplementary Activities

Following each lesson are one or more Supplementary Activities designed to appeal to students of varying abilities. These activities will help students process the ideas presented in the lesson and provide opportunities for them to practice targeted skills.

Scheduling the Lessons

Lessons should last 30-45 minutes, depending on your students' attention spans. Some lessons can be divided and taught in segments without undermining their effectiveness. Teaching the lesson early in the school day will allow you to capitalize on opportunities during the remainder of the day to use lesson vocabulary and to encourage students to use skills that were introduced that morning.

Because every school and classroom has its own particular set of characteristics, you will want to utilize the materials included here in your own unique way. Some teachers integrate lessons into their health, social studies, and language arts/communication curricula. Others set up a formal "social skills" period and teach lessons once per week or use a "unit" format, teaching a lesson or doing an activity on a daily basis for a period of time. Some teachers prefer to introduce this material more casually, teaching a lesson from time to time when they see a need for instruction in a specific skill. Still others weave lesson concepts and activities into their art and creative writing programs or into integrated units in the content areas.

You can achieve maximum results with this curriculum by finding ways for students to practice and review the concepts regularly and by consistently extending the learning to other areas throughout the school year. Be alert for teachable moments—times at which you can verbally link present events to self-esteem concepts you have taught. Just as a single vitamin tablet administered on a regular basis is a more effective regimen than a handful once per month, social skill training responds well to small, consistent skill applications.

You will find that students enjoy repeating some of the games and that there are a number of ways to vary activities for additional practice. A particularly effective technique for achieving transfer of training involves asking students to write down or explain a specific time when they will implement a behavior that is encouraged in the lesson. Follow-up might involve asking students to write you a note or to indicate on a class chart when they used the behavior. This type of consistent reinforcement will not only combat the tendency of new learning to fade with time but will model for students that you are genuinely interested in them as people who have needs and concerns beyond the realm of academics.

Using the Technique of Class Discussion to Teach Personal/Social Skills

Class discussion is a valuable teaching tool, especially when the discussion is structured so that students who are functioning on a high personal/social level can share their knowledge, experience, and opinions with their peers. Studies have shown that even at the kindergarten level students are influenced more by the comments of peers than by the comments of their teacher.

Following are some suggestions to make class discussion more effective:

- If possible, seat students in a circle or horseshoe shape so they can all see each other.
- Ask open-ended questions such as, "What can you tell us about . . . ?" or "Can you tell us more about . . . ?"
- If a student who is not attending well is not ready to give a response to a question, say you will come back to him or her shortly for a response.
- If a student is dominating the discussion, say something like, "We have to move on, but I would be interested in hearing more later."
- Use the technique of "thumbs up or down" to get all students to respond to general questions.
- Remember that repeating a question after you call on a student will train the students to not listen to you.
- Encourage students to give complete answers; refrain from repeating or elaborating on their answers for them.
- Encourage discussion and avoid giving "sermonettes" about lesson topics.
- Structure discussion to encourage students with high social functioning to suggest examples of the concepts you are presenting.

Suggestions for Enhancing the Teaching of This Curriculum

- Assign students a "Learning Partner" with whom they can discuss lesson concepts when you direct them to do so.
- Emphasize the fun activities that accompany each lesson.
- Supply students with a "think pad" to write on during lessons.
- Make sure students keep all handouts and materials from the lessons in a folder.
- Instead of trying to complete lessons in a given time, let students' interests, responses, needs, and contributions shape the lessons.
- Incorporate vocabulary lists and writing activities from the lessons into your language arts program.
- Send home the parent letters included in the units.
- Make notes about lesson content on index cards for reference as you teach from the lesson transparencies.
- Make audiotapes of the lessons and listen to them on your way to or from school to familiarize yourself with lesson content. Having done so, you can extemporize much of the lesson as you show students the transparencies.

Helping Kids Handle Put-Downs

Primary Version

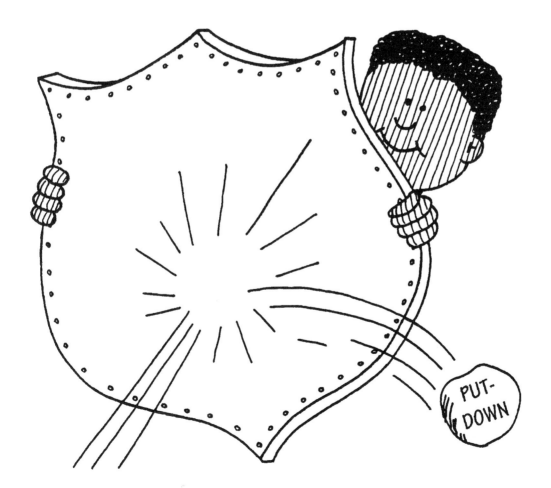

Introduction to Primary Lessons

In these lessons students learn how to handle put-downs by ignoring them, by using their imagination to deflect them, by using agreeing responses, and by giving "crazy compliments." In addition they learn to use self-encouragement to keep put-downs from damaging their self-esteem. They also learn about the negative effect put-downs have on friendships and are given some techniques for stopping themselves from giving put-downs when they are tempted to do so.

Kindergarteners and first graders will benefit most from Lesson 1 (teaching the ignoring technique), Lesson 2 (teaching the imagination technique), Lesson 4 (teaching the self-encouragement technique), and Lesson 5 (teaching students how to stop themselves from giving put-downs). All of the primary lessons can be used with older primary students (grades 2 and 3). At the end of each lesson are one or more Supplementary Activities that can be used for reinforcement of the lesson concepts.

Following this Introduction is a letter to parents and guardians regarding ways they can help their children deal with put-downs. This letter informs parents and guardians of the goals of the unit and provides information to help them teach as well as reinforce unit skills and concepts. K-1 teachers will want to send home only that portion of the letter that refers to the skills they are teaching.

Finally, you may extend the lessons by reading to your class one or more of the fiction books about teasing or put-downs from the list at the end of this Introduction.

Parent/Guardian Letter

Dear Parent/Guardian:

I am writing to ask your support as we begin a unit in our classroom on assertive strategies for handling put-downs. Even though we try to prevent put-downs, they are a fact of school life. When they occur, many children chant, "Sticks and stones may break my bones, but words will never hurt me," or "I'm rubber and you're glue; whatever you say bounces off me and sticks to you," but put-downs are still painful and can be devastating to self-esteem. The following is a synopsis of the techniques for handling put-downs that your child will be learning in the classroom. You can help to maximize your child's learning by guiding him or her through real or imaginary situations where your child can practice using these strategies.

Many children need a large repertoire of strategies in order to hold their own in a variety of social conflict situations. The first technique we will be working on is **ignoring**. With this technique, the child holds his or her head high and affects a nonchalant body posture that implies, "You haven't hurt me with your put-down." With training, practice, and self-confidence, ignoring can become an art.

When faced with particularly hurtful comments, children can learn to **use their imaginations** to visualize put-downs bouncing off them or whizzing right past them. Some children imagine they have an invisible shield that wards off put-downs. Others like to imagine that they're karate experts who can simply jump aside and let a put-down fly past them or who can smash the put-down with a single karate chop. A favorite image of children is to imagine wearing a bulletproof vest which keeps put-downs from "penetrating their hearts."

Many children find that, to save face, they need to say something when they receive a put-down. We will be focusing on some assertive verbal responses to put-downs which do not incite retaliation and which also tend to invite respect and leave the door open for the possibility of friendship. These responses fall into two categories: agreeing with the put-down and giving a crazy compliment. Both types allow a child to respond to a put-down without returning the insult and escalating the verbal conflict.

While the response of **agreeing with a put-down** may seem foreign, it doesn't imply that your child really agrees with the attacker or the put-down. It is merely an effective way for your child to surprise the aggressor, allowing your child to feel strong and composed. Students have identified the following examples of agreeing statements as their favorites:

- Amazing, but true!
- Hard to believe, isn't it?
- Nice of you to notice.
- That was supposed to be a secret!
- That's an interesting way to look at it.
- Wasn't that a great mistake?
- Disgusting, isn't it?
- That's life!
- Yep, that's me all over!

Another powerful way to deal with a put-down from a peer is to **give a "crazy compliment."** Crazy compliments tell the put-downer that his or her put-down had little effect and in fact may not even have been understood as a put-down! Many students enjoy using the following kinds of crazy compliments:

- Nice eyebrows!
- You have great ears!
- Nice shoulders!
- Nice elbows!
- I like your tonsils.
- You have great arms. I like your left one even better than your right!

Finally, you can give a gift for life by encouraging your child to **talk to himself or herself as a good friend would** when he or she is hurting from a put-down. Making positive and truthful self-statements can keep your child from dwelling on hurtful comments. By reminding themselves of their strengths and good qualities, children can sustain their self-esteem at an especially vulnerable moment. Many students have found the following self-statements helpful in keeping put-downs from hurting:

- I know I'm a neat kid.
- Other people like me.
- They don't know what I'm really like.
- No matter what they say, I'm O.K.
- I'm not going to let this bother me.
- I know I'm a good person.
- He only sees me on the outside.
- She's just trying to impress the other kids.

By encouraging your child to ignore, agree with, or give "crazy compliments" in response to put-downs, or to use his or her imagination to deflect insults, you will enable him or her to be assertive (rather than aggressive or passive) with peers. By reminding your child to use the self-care technique of self-encouragement, you will enable him or her to keep put-downs from eroding self-esteem.

Sincerely,

Keeping in Touch

Date _____

Dear Parent/Guardian,

In our classroom your child is learning:

Your child's homework this week is:

If you wish, you can help by:

If you have any questions or concerns, please call me at:

Thank you for your support.

Sincerely,

Primary Fiction Books on Teasing and Put-Downs

Cohen, B. (1983). *Molly's pilgrim.* New York: Lothrop, Lee and Shepard.

Crary, E. (1996). *My Name Is Not Dummy.* Seattle: Parent Press.

DePaola, T. (1979). *Oliver Button is a sissy.* Orlando: Harcourt Brace Jovanovich.

Dussling, J. (1996). *Don't Call Me Names: Have You Ever Been Teased?* New York: Grosset & Dunlap.

Grant, E. (1980). *I hate my name.* Chatham, NJ: Steck-Vaughan Publishing.

Henkes, K. (1988). *Chrysanthemum.* New York: Greenwillow Books.

Hogan, P.Z. (1980). *I hate boys and I hate girls.* Chatham, NJ: Steck-Vaughan Publishing.

Hurwitz, J. (1979). *Aldo applesauce.* New York: William Morrow and Co.

Lasker, J. (1982). *The do-something day.* New York: Scholastic.

Reider, K. (1997). *Snail Started It!* New York: North-South Books.

Vesey, A. (1993). *Hector's new sneakers.* New York: Penguin Press.

Waber, B. (1976). *But names will never hurt me.* Boston: Houghton Mifflin.

Yashima, T. (1955). *Crow boy.* New York: Viking.

Why Kids Give Put-Downs and How to Ignore Them

Objective   Students will learn some reasons behind put-down behavior, as well as the fact that giving put-downs can cause others to not trust them.

Students will learn the technique of ignoring put-downs to mitigate the hurt that put-downs can cause.

Materials   Transparency #1 – "Put-Downs Hurt Friendships"

Transparency #2 – "Why Kids Give Put-Downs—1"

Transparency #3 – "Different Is O.K."

Transparency #4 – "Why Kids Give Put-Downs—2"

Transparency #5 – "Why Kids Give Put-Downs—3"

Transparency #6 – "Kids Don't Trust a Put-Downer"

Transparency #7 – "Stop and Think: Do I REALLY Want to Be a Put-Downer?"

Transparency #8 – "'Sticks and Stones May Break My Bones, But Words Will Never Hurt Me'—Not True!"

Transparency #9 – "Put-Downs Can Hurt Just As Much"

Transparency #10 – "Dumped-On Dinah"

Transparency #11 – "Ignoring Put-Downs: Giving the 'Long, Cool Look'"

Teacher Sheet – "Insult Bank for Guided Practice"

Transparency #12 – "Put-Downs for Practice"

Poster #1 – "Don't Give Put-Downs"

Poster #2/Handout #1 – "Keeping Count"

Puppet for teacher

Puppets, or socks to use as puppets, for students (optional)

Transparency marker

To the Teacher

In almost every classroom a certain amount of teasing occurs, and some students find themselves the object of derision or ridicule. The question arises as to why students make cruel comments to one another. There seem to be a variety of reasons.

It appears that some students use put-downs as an attempt to impress other students and gain status in a group. Most students are less cruel in a one-on-one situation than they are when they have an audience. Teasing may also stem from a desire to strike out because of some personal hurt or deprivation. Sometimes put-downs are habitual outlets for minor irritations or embarrassment. In other instances, ridicule appears to be a way in which children socialize with one another. Many students appear to be bludgeoning one another into social conformity with put-downs.

Whatever the underlying causes, put-downs and teasing have the potential to seriously erode self-esteem. It is hard for students to like themselves when peers, whose opinions are important, say critical things about them. Not knowing how to respond to put-downs can cause students to feel helpless and incompetent. These negative feelings may persist long after the put-downs have stopped. All students need to learn the assertive skill of handling teasing calmly and with a quiet confidence rather than in a hostile, aggressive manner.

Students who are particularly deficient in this skill often seem to attract and even encourage ridicule. By fighting back, lashing out in anger, crying, or tattling, they give their attackers the reaction they want. These students need to understand that this kind of reinforcing behavior is partly to blame for the number of put-downs they receive. They need to expand their repertoire of responses to teasing and put-downs so that they don't become entrenched in a victim role. Teasing can be the same as a "put-down" if the victim doesn't like or feels hurt by what is said.

Lesson Presentation

Transp. #1

Put Transparency #1, "Put-Downs Hurt Friendships," on the overhead. **A put-down is something someone says to someone else that makes the person feel bad. A put-down can be calling others a name they don't like, like "Hey, Dog-Face!" or "Look out! Here comes Bigfoot!"** *Write "name-calling" on the transparency.* **Another kind of put-down is making fun of others when they can't do something very well—laughing at their drawing or saying things when they miss a word in reading or strike out in baseball.** *Write "making fun of others" on the transparency.* **Getting a put-down is kind of like having someone thrust a knife in your heart. A knife hurts on the outside; a put-down hurts on the inside.** *Point to the knife on transparency.*

Kids, of course, don't want to be friends with someone who physically hurts them. They also don't want to be friends with someone who puts them down or insults them. Today we're going to talk about why some kids like to give put-downs and how a put-downer can stop giving put-downs.

SOME PEOPLE PUT DOWN OTHERS WHO ARE DIFFERENT FROM THEM

Transp. #2

There are lots of reasons why one kid will put another kid down. Sometimes kids will put someone down because that person is different from them. *Put Transparency #2, "Why Kids Give Put-Downs—1," on the overhead. Point out the way the boy on the left is making fun of the boy on the right because he's different from him.* **Maybe the boy on the right comes from a different country or a different part of the United States, and maybe he dresses differently or talks with a different accent. Maybe he does things differently because of his religion or because his family has some different customs. Maybe his hair is extra curly, or maybe he's different from the boy on the left simply because he loves to draw but can't seem to memorize his math facts.**

Transp. #3

Kids need to realize that different is O.K. There's not just one right way to be. Just because some people don't look the way you think they should doesn't mean they don't look good. Different from you is O.K.! *(Show Transparency # 3, "Different Is O.K.")* **All people have a right to be the way they are. No one deserves a put-down because of being different from you.**

SOME PUT-DOWNERS HAVE BEEN TREATED BADLY THEMSELVES

Transp. #4

There's another reason kids put other kids down. *Place Transparency #4, "Why Kids Give Put-Downs—2," on the overhead.* **Sometimes when a kid has been put down by someone, he or she will give a put-down to someone else.** *Explain the pass-the-put-down sequence shown on the transparency.* **When someone gives us a put-down, we get in a bad mood, don't we? Sometimes when we're in a bad mood, we feel like blasting everybody in sight! Some kids have grown up in homes where people have a habit of saying mean things to one another. They feel in a bad mood a lot of the time. They've gotten into the habit of being mean because that is the way they have been treated. When I hear somebody give a put-down, I sometimes think to myself, "I wonder if they have had their feelings hurt a lot." How many of you have wondered the same thing?** *Ask for a show of hands.*

SOME KIDS THINK BEING A PUT-DOWNER MAKES THEM STRONG OR POPULAR

Transp. #5

There's another reason kids give put-downs, and I think this is the reason for most put-downs. Some kids just don't like themselves very much, and one way they try to feel better is by putting other kids down. *Put Transparency #5, "Why Kids Give Put-Downs—3," on the overhead.* Here you see two kids. The one on the left, Kid A, is picking on Kid B. It may be that she wants to feel bigger and more powerful than Kid B. *Point at the figures on the transparency.* Or she may be putting Kid B down because she thinks her put-downs will make her more popular with the other kids. Put-downers think that if they can get other kids to laugh at their put-downs, the other kids will like them more. When you hear a kid putting down another kid, how do you feel about it? Does it make you like the put-downer more? *Allow for student input.* When a put-downer picks on somebody, do you think, "Wow! That put-downer is really a neat kid!" *Allow for student response.*

KIDS DON'T REALLY TRUST A PUT-DOWNER

Transp. #6

A put-downer wants <u>really badly</u> to be noticed and liked. But do you know what is sad about a put-downer? *Put Transparency #6, "Kids Don't Trust a Put-Downer," on the overhead.* Other kids don't really <u>trust</u> a put-downer. They may laugh at the put-down, but on the inside they don't trust the put-downer. They know they may be the next one the put-downer insults. *Read and explain the cartoon on the transparency.*

Transp. #7

I think everyone in our class wants to have friends and be liked. But none of us is perfect, and some of us will give put-downs from time to time. If you find yourself giving other kids put-downs, you need to STOP and THINK. *Put Transparency #7, "Stop and Think: Do I REALLY Want to Be a Put-Downer?" on the overhead.* Do you want everyone to see that you're mean? Are the few laughs you'll get for your put-down worth it if people don't trust you?

PUT-DOWNS HURT

**Transp. #8
Transp. #9**

We've all heard the saying, "Sticks and stones may break my bones, but words will never hurt me." But words can hurt, can't they? *Show Transparency #8, "'Sticks and Stones May Break My Bones, But Words Will*

Never Hurt Me'—Not True!" **Insulting words can hurt a lot.** *Read the put-downs on the transparency aloud.* **It's not true that words can't hurt. The put-downs these kids are giving this boy hurt his feelings a lot.** *Show Transparency #9, "Put-Downs Can Hurt Just As Much."* **He even tells himself that what they are saying is true—that he does have a funny-looking body, big ears, big teeth, and the wrong style haircut.** *Read aloud the words in the thought bubble and point out the view the boy has of himself.* **Give a thumbs-up if you think getting a put-down would hurt <u>your</u> feelings.**

By the end of this lesson, you'll know some ways to keep put-downs from hurting so much, and how to not give put-downers what they want.

SOME KIDS BRING PUT-DOWNS ON THEMSELVES

Transp. #10

Some kids bring put-downs on themselves. Let me show you what I mean. *Put Transparency #10, "Dumped-On Dinah," on the overhead.* **Here's a girl, Dumped-On Dinah, who gets tons of put-downs because she gives put-downers just what they want. When someone gives her a put-down, she shows she's really upset. Sometimes she shows this by crying. Sometimes she tattles on the put-downer. Sometimes she screams a bunch of put-downs back, hoping to say something even meaner than what the put-downer said to her. But all of these responses guarantee that the put-downer will keep calling her names. If Dinah knew the tricks that you're going to learn today, she could get most kids to stop insulting her. The put-downers would be very impressed by her coolness.**

USING THE IGNORING TECHNIQUE WITH PUT-DOWNS

The first trick you can use when someone gives you a put-down is to IGNORE the put-down. I know it's hard not to react to a put-down, and I don't mean that you shouldn't react at all. Ignoring a put-down means not reacting to it in the way the put-downer wants you to. It means not acting like you're hurt or mad. Let me show you what I mean.

Transp. #11 puppet(s)

Show Transparency #11, "Ignoring Put-Downs: Giving the 'Long, Cool Look.'" Give students time to read the transparency and then hold up a puppet. Say or paraphrase: **Who'll volunteer to use this puppet and give me a put-down about the clothes I'm wearing today?** *Call on a student volunteer. Have the student use the puppet to depersonalize the put-down. After the put-down is delivered, model stopping what you're doing, looking the puppet straight in the eye in an assertive manner for at least three seconds, and then going back to what you were doing.*

Do you get the idea? You don't say a thing. Instead, you sit or stand up tall and proud, and you give the person a long, cool look. *(Model this.)* **You don't act hurt or scared, just strong and calm. How do you think a put-downer would feel about how I reacted to the put-down?** *Allow for student response.* **Of course, you can also ignore a put-down by not even looking at the person—by acting like you're not even thinking of him or her. But some kids like to give that long, cool look so the put-downer will see that he or she didn't get to them.**

PRACTICING THE IGNORING TECHNIQUE

Teacher Sheet

You can learn to do this, too. Let's have a couple of volunteers model the ignoring technique. *Choose two volunteers and designate one as the "put-downer" and the other as the "ignorer." Assign the put-downer a nonthreatening area to insult, such as drawing ability, cutting and pasting skills, the tidiness of a student's desk and belongings, the kind of lunch a student brings, etc. (Or you may want to choose a put-down from the Teacher Sheet "Insult Bank for Guided Practice" and whisper the put-down to the volunteer. In both cases, be sure to avoid sensitive areas for specific students.)*

Have the put-downer use a puppet to depersonalize the insult. Remind the "ignorer" to stand tall, look strong and proud, and give the puppet a long, cool look. Choose several pairs of students to model this technique until you feel the students have grasped the concept.

Transp. #12

Good job! When you ignore a put-down, it's as if you're saying, "Your put-down doesn't matter to me—it doesn't bother me at all." Now I want everyone to have a chance to practice ignoring put-downs. Let's practice the ignoring technique with puppets. I'd like you to use these put-downs on the transparency. *Put Transparency #12, "Put-Downs for Practice," on the overhead. (You may wish to read the put-downs* *aloud to very young students.)* Then divide the class into Learning Partner pairs and say, **Turn to your Learning Partner and see which of you is shorter. Let's have the shorter person use the puppet** *(or sock or hand)* **to give a put-down and the taller person practice ignoring the put-down. Then switch and have the taller person give the put-down.**

Again, puppets are used to depersonalize the put-downs. They can be hand puppets or a sock slipped over the hand. An even simpler alternative is to have the put-downers use their <u>bare hands</u> as if they were puppets, opening and closing the thumb against the other fingers as if their hand were a talking mouth.

After a few minutes, debrief the experience, asking such questions as: **When you were the put-downer, how did you feel about being ignored? When you were being insulted, how did it feel to use the long, cool look? Do you think this technique would work for you? Can you think of a time you could have used it in the past?**

Summarize by saying: **We can ignore put-downs to stop them from "getting to us."**

A CLASS SAFE FROM PUT-DOWNS

Poster #1

I hope you will all use the ignoring technique the next time someone puts you down. I hope even more that our classroom will be a place where everyone is <u>safe</u> from put-downs. I'm going to hang up a poster as a reminder to all of us. *Show students Poster #1, "Don't Give Put-Downs."*

I'd also like you to begin to notice when you hear a put-down, whether it's said to you or to someone else, and to say to the put-downer, "Hey, that's a put-down," in a calm voice. That will remind people that we don't give put-downs in our classroom.

NICKNAMES AND LAUGHING AT EACH OTHER'S MISTAKES COUNT AS PUT-DOWNS, TOO

Engage students in a discussion regarding how they feel when people laugh at them when they make a mistake. Then ask if any students have nicknames they resent being called (but have them avoid mentioning what these nicknames *are if they are not already known to their classmates). Explain that unless you know <u>for sure</u> that a person likes a nickname, you shouldn't use it. Encourage class agreement that these two behaviors usually fall under the category of being a put-down.*

KEEPING COUNT OF PUT-DOWNS AND FRIENDLY COMMENTS IN THE CLASS AS A WHOLE

**Poster #2
Handout #1**

If we want to make our class a friendlier place, one in which everyone feels accepted, we're going to have to make it safe from put-downs. One way we can do this is to keep track of any put-downs we hear, as well as all of the friendly comments. Then we can see if we can give more friendly comments than put-downs. *You may wish to assign two or three "Tally Kids" each day to keep track of put-downs and friendly comments on their own tally sheets (Handout #1, "Keeping Count"). Then you can take an average of their counts at the end of each day and write these totals on the class poster (Poster #2, "Keeping Count").*

Another way to keep this count is to appoint five students to be "Put-Down Monitors" and have them tally the put-downs and friendly comments they hear on an enlarged version of the class poster that you've hung up in the classroom. To minimize class disruption, allow them to go to the poster only at selected times during the day. (Since there may be some duplication of observations using this method, adjust the count if you feel it necessary.)

At the end of each day, talk with the class about the number of put-downs and friendly comments recorded for that day. Tell the students that you expect that, as the days go by, there will be fewer and fewer put-downs. Continue to keep this tally for two or three weeks, and compare the results from week to week. Make a large graph comparing the number of put-downs to positive comments as the days go by. You may wish to reward the class with an extra art period, free-choice time, or an extra recess if they show an increase in friendly comments and a decrease in put-downs.

LESSON REVIEW

Review the lesson by having students respond verbally to one or more of the following sentence stems:

- *I learned . . . .*

- *I was surprised . . . .*

- *I liked . . . .*

- *I will try . . . .*

STUDENTS TALLY AND GRAPH THEIR OWN PUT-DOWNS AND FRIENDLY COMMENTS

For a portion of time each day have students keep track of any put-downs or positive comments they give using Handout #1, "Keeping Count." Show them how to graph these counts on a bar or line graph. Watching their put-downs decrease and their positive interactions increase is a powerful motivator for behavior change and learning.

SUPPLEMENTARY ACTIVITIES

Use the Supplementary Activities that follow this lesson to reinforce lesson concepts:

- *"Put-Down Spaghetti"*
  (Supplementary Activity #1)

- *"Using Role-Plays to Practice Ignoring Put-Downs (Second Grade)"*
  (Supplementary Activity #2)

- *"Using Role-Plays to Practice Ignoring Put-Downs (Third Grade)"*
  (Supplementary Activity #3)

TRANSPARENCY #1

Put-Downs Hurt Friendships

TRANSPARENCY #2

Why Kids Give Put-Downs

1.
Because someone is different from them.

TRANSPARENCY #3

Different Is O.K.

TRANSPARENCY #4

Why Kids Give Put-Downs

2.
Because they got one.

TRANSPARENCY #5

Why Kids Give Put-Downs

3.

To try to look big or impress other kids.

Kid A   Kid B

TRANSPARENCY #6

Kids Don't Trust a Put-Downer

TRANSPARENCY #7

Stop and Think: "Do I REALLY Want to Be a Put-Downer?"

TRANSPARENCY #8

"Sticks and Stones May Break My Bones, But Words Will Never Hurt Me"—Not True!

TRANSPARENCY #9

Put-Downs
Can Hurt Just As Much

TRANSPARENCY #10

Dumped-On Dinah

TRANSPARENCY #11

Ignoring Put-Downs: Giving the "Long, Cool Look"

A powerful thing to do when you get a put-down is to not say anything and follow these steps.

Step 1:   Sit or stand up straight.

Step 2:   Hold your head high.

Step 3:   Look at the person.

Step 4:   Go back to what you were doing.

TEACHER SHEET

Insult Bank for Guided Practice

Have students you designate as put-downers use a puppet to deliver these put-downs to other students. The use of the puppet will help prevent the students from taking the insults personally. Explain that it would be really mean and very unfair for students to use insults like these to hurt others.

- Get lost, Ugly!

- I like your funny hat—oh, sorry, that's your hair, isn't it?

- Hey, Pencil-Neck!

- Hey, did you escape from the zoo?

- Hey, Dumbo. Give me some of your snack.

- Would you like one of the kindergartners to help you with that?

- Do we laugh now or when you talk?

- Hey, Clumsy! Nice move!

- No one's listening to you, Motor-Mouth!

- You're so stupid, I hear you even flunked recess.

- You should wear a sign on your head that says, "Help Wanted."

- Is that your lunch, or are you taking out the garbage?

- Oh, oh—looks like your mommy forgot to pack your bottle!

- You eat like a pig with hiccups.

- Is the other team paying you to be so crummy?

- My dog can catch better than you can.

- Even a skunk would think you stink.

- I wish you were on TV so I could turn you off.

- People like you don't grow on trees—they swing from them.

- You should go to Hollywood. The walk will do you good.

- Do you take dork lessons, or does acting like a dork just come naturally?

- Last time I saw a face like yours, I threw it a fish!

- You're so ugly your nose hangs down to your toes.

- You look like Bozo the Clown.

- Do you take **ugly pills**, or what?

- I see you found your shirt after the dog tried to bury it again, huh?

- Is that what all the **preschoolers** are wearing this year?

- Your mother sure dresses you funny.

TRANSPARENCY #12

Put-Downs for Practice

1. You're so dumb you can't add 2 + 2.

2. Hey, Klutz! Can't you walk two feet without tripping?

3. Your breath smells gross.

4. Your hair looks really dumb.

5. My dog can catch better than you!

6. Your shirt looks really dumb.

POSTER #1

POSTER #2/HANDOUT #1

Keeping Count

	Put-Downs	**Friendly Comments**
1		
Monday		
Tuesday		
Wednesday		
Thursday		
Friday		
2		
Monday		
Tuesday		
Wednesday		
Thursday		
Friday		
3		
Monday		
Tuesday		
Wednesday		
Thursday		
Friday		

SUPPLEMENTARY ACTIVITY #1

Put-Down Spaghetti

This tangled-up piece of spaghetti has a message in it that will tell you one of the best ways to handle a put-down. To find out the message, color in the circles that have a *. Then, follow along the spaghetti. Every time you come to a colored circle, write the letter in it on the line at the bottom of the page.

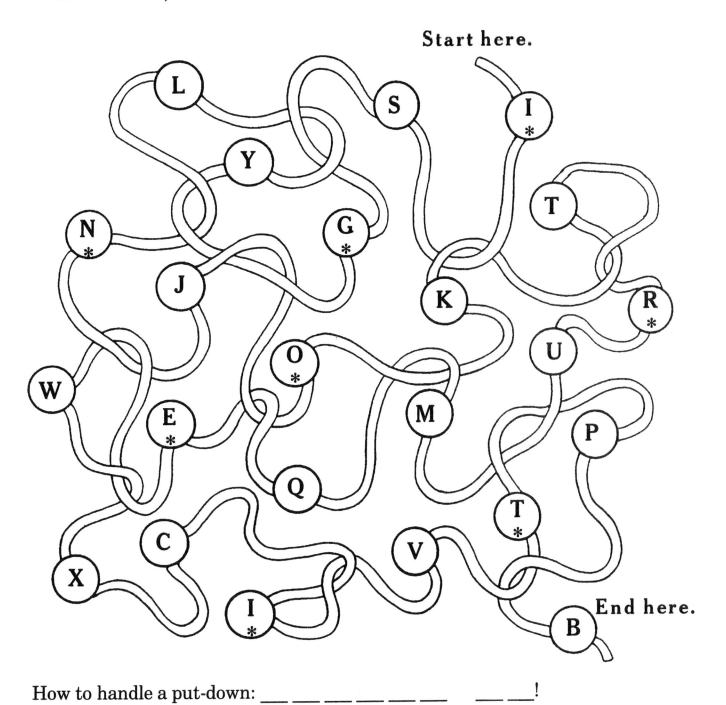

Start here.

End here.

How to handle a put-down: __ __ __ __ __ __   __ __!

SUPPLEMENTARY ACTIVITY #2

Using Role-Plays to Practice Ignoring Put-Downs (Second Grade)

Objective   Students will practice ignoring put-downs from their peers.

Materials   Transparency #11 from the lesson, "Ignoring Put-Downs: Giving the 'Long, Cool Look'"

Supplementary Activity #2 Teacher Sheet, "Cards for Ignoring Put-Downs" (cut the cards apart; you'll need one card for each student)

Puppets

Procedure   Using Transparency #11 from the lesson, review with the class the technique of ignoring put-downs. Discuss or model appropriate body language that conveys to others that a put-down had no effect. Then ask for a student volunteer to model the ignoring technique. Use a hand puppet to deliver a put-down to the student volunteer. Ask the class to identify the ignoring behaviors they saw modeled by the student volunteer. Continue to review in this manner until the class seems ready to practice the technique on their own.

Next, divide the class into Learning Partner pairs. Have the Learning Partners face one another and take turns in the roles of the "put-downer" and the "ignorer." Have each put-downer draw a Put-Down Card and read it aloud to his or her partner. (To depersonalize the put-down, you may wish to have the put-downers use puppets, or use their hands as puppets, to deliver the put-downs.) The other partner will role-play ignoring behavior. Then have partners switch roles and draw a new card.

Alternatively, it may be useful to have Learning Partners role-play giving and receiving the insult on their Put-Down Cards for the rest of the class, one pair of partners at a time.

Nice going, Liver-Lips! You made us lose the game!

My pet canary can do math better than you can!

SUPPLEMENTARY ACTIVITY #2 TEACHER SHEET

Cards for Ignoring Put-Downs

Hey, nice to see you, Monkey-Brain!	Hi-ya, Carrot-Nose!
If you were any slower, a turtle would leave you in the dust!	What a baby! Where's your bottle?
You dropped the ball, Butterfingers! What a dork!	Who picked out your clothes— your little brother?
My little sister can read better than you can! **Duh!**	Guess who you eat like— Oink! Oink!
You're so dumb, you probably failed kindergarten!	You sure are funny looking!
Are those your regular clothes, or are you practicing to be a clown when you grow up?	My pet canary can do math better than you can!
Nice going, Liver-Lips! You made us lose the game!	My dog's better looking than you are!
If I had hair like yours, I'd shave it off!	You were absent yesterday. Sorry you're back!

SUPPLEMENTARY ACTIVITY #3

Using Role-Plays to Practice Ignoring Put-Downs (Third Grade)

Objective   Students will practice ignoring put-downs from their peers.

Materials   Transparency #11 from the lesson, "Ignoring Put-Downs: Giving the 'Long, Cool Look'"

Supplementary Activity #3 Teacher Sheet, "Cards for Ignoring Put-Downs" (cut the cards apart; you'll need one card for each student)

Puppets

Procedure   Using Transparency #11 from the lesson, review with the class the technique of ignoring put-downs. Discuss or model appropriate body language that conveys to others that a put-down had no effect. Then ask for a student volunteer to model the ignoring technique. Use a hand puppet to deliver a put-down to the student volunteer. Ask the class to identify the ignoring behaviors they saw modeled by the student volunteer. Continue to review in this manner until the class seems ready to practice the technique on their own.

Next, divide the class into Learning Partner pairs. Have the Learning Partners face one another and take turns in the roles of the "put-downer" and the "ignorer." Have each put-downer draw a Put-Down Card and read it aloud to his or her partner. (To depersonalize the put-down, you may wish to have the put-downers use puppets, or use their hands as puppets, to deliver the put-downs.) The other partner will role-play ignoring behavior. Then have partners switch roles and draw a new card.

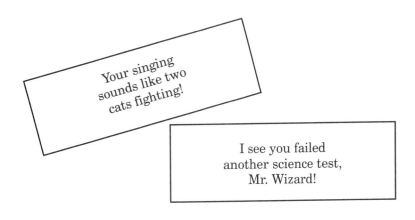

SUPPLEMENTARY ACTIVITY #3 TEACHER SHEET

Cards for Ignoring Put-Downs

Your feet are so big, you have to throw the shoes away and wear the boxes!	If I give you my lunch, will you promise to put the bag over your head?
Why don't you make like a tree and leave?	You set a new record at recess. I never saw anyone strike out as many times as you did!
Did you cut your hair yourself, or is it just naturally funny looking?	I see you failed another science test, Mr. Wizard!
You sure do have a lot of muscles— too bad they're all in your head!	Nice outfit! I saw something just like it— last Halloween!
Close your mouth— you'll let the flies out!	Hey, Klutz! Do us a favor and play on the other team so we can win!
You should be in the movies— you'd make a great Godzilla!	I think I saw one of your cousins last weekend— it was in the Monkey House at the zoo!
Your singing sounds like two cats fighting!	What a slob! You should wear a bib when you eat!
What are you going to be when you grow up? A trained monkey?	Hi-ya, Brainless! Failed any math tests lately?

How to Keep Put-Downs
From Hurting Self-Esteem: Using Imagination

Objective   Students will learn the technique of using their imaginations to mitigate the hurt that put-downs can cause.

Materials   Transparency #10 from Lesson 1 – "Dumped-On Dinah"

Transparency #11 from Lesson 1 – "Ignoring Put-Downs: Giving the 'Long, Cool Look'"

Transparency #1 – "What to Imagine When You Get a Put-Down"

Transparency #2/Poster #1 – "Techniques to Use With Put-Downers"

Handout #1 from Lesson 1 – "Keeping Count"

To the Teacher

In Lesson 1, students learned some reasons behind put-down behavior and the nonverbal technique of ignoring put-downs to mitigate the hurt that put-downs can cause. Lesson 2 builds on the work of the previous lesson by teaching students a technique to use after ignoring a put-down—deflecting the put-down through the use of imagination. Students will practice imagining that they have a shield, bulletproof vest, or karate move to protect themselves against the harm of put-downs. Through this use of imagination students will be able to keep themselves from ruminating on unkind remarks.

Students should be encouraged to practice this and the ignoring technique as well as to continue to monitor the put-downs and positive comments they make to others through the chart provided in Lesson 1.

Lesson Presentation

REVIEW OF THE PREVIOUS LESSON

Remember "Dumped-On Dinah" from our last lesson? *Show Transparency #10 from Lesson 1.* **Why was she feeling so upset?** *Allow for student response.* **That's right. Kids were putting her down. In our last lesson you learned one powerful technique that Dinah and the rest of us could use to get most kids to stop insulting her. If you remember what that special trick was, give a thumbs-up.** *Call on one person to describe the technique. Then show Transparency #11 from Lesson 1, "Ignoring Put-Downs: Giving the 'Long, Cool Look'" and review the steps listed.*

USING YOUR IMAGINATION WHEN YOU GET A PUT-DOWN

Transp. #1

Ignoring is a great technique, but I know it's not easy to just ignore put-downs. It hurts when you're called names. Sometimes a put-down feels like a knife that goes right into your heart. Let me tell you about another trick that some kids use right after they ignore a put-down trick to keep the put-down from hurting so much. It involves using your imagination. *Put Transparency #1, "What to Imagine When You Get a Put-Down," on the overhead, covering the three examples so they can be revealed one at a time.*

We can use our imaginations to help us when someone tries to put us down. Let's play an imagination game. Look at this picture on the overhead. *Uncover the shield picture, but keep the other pictures covered.* **First, we're going to imagine that we have an invisible shield we can hold up so that put-downs bounce right off us.**

IMAGINING HOLDING AN INVISIBLE SHIELD

Are you ready to play the imagination game? Think of a time when someone gave you a put-down—a time when an invisible shield would have helped. *Pause.* **Remember what the put-downer said.** *Pause.* **Now imagine you were holding a big shield that no one could see but you.** *Pause.* **When the person threw that put-down at you, it bounced right off your shield and fell onto the ground. Imagine the look of surprise on the put-downer's face when you weren't affected by the put-down!** *Pause.* **Were you able to imagine it? How did it feel to have the put-down bounce off?** *Allow for student response.*

IMAGINING BEING A KARATE EXPERT

Uncover the karate picture. **Now, look up here again. Another way we can use our imaginations is to think of ourselves as skillful karate experts. We can, in our minds, jump aside so that a put-down misses us or give the put-down a karate chop as it comes at us. Of course, none of us would imagine giving a karate chop to the <u>person</u> who gives the put-down, because we're not mean. We're just protecting ourselves by imagining blasting the put-down itself.**

Let's practice imagining ourselves using a karate move on a put-down. First, let's imagine jumping aside and letting the put-down whiz by.

Think of another time when someone gave you a put-down. *Pause.* Now imagine you are standing in front of that put-downer, and you have on a white karate jacket and pants. You're wearing a black belt—you're one of the best! *Pause.* Imagine that person throwing the put-down at you. . . . Here it comes. *Pause.* Quick as a flash, you jump aside! *Pause.* The put-down whizzes past you and disappears behind you! *Pause.* How did you feel watching the put-down whiz past you? *Allow for student response.*

Now let's imagine karate-chopping the put-down. Imagine you're wearing your karate outfit. *Pause.* See in your mind the person who is about to give you a put-down . . . and here comes the put-down like a big rock coming at you! *Pause.* With one quick karate chop, you smash it into tiny pieces! *Pause.* Notice how good it feels to stop a put-down from hitting you. *Pause.* How did you like imagining this? *Allow for student response.*

IMAGINING WEARING A BULLETPROOF VEST

Let me tell you about one last thing you might want to imagine. *Uncover the bulletproof vest picture.* Look at this kid who's wearing a bulletproof vest. *Point to the transparency again.* Try to imagine that it's you who's wearing a bulletproof vest. In a minute I'm going to ask you to imagine a put-down heading right for your heart . . . only it can't pierce your heart and hurt you because you're wearing the vest. Instead, the put-down will bounce off your bulletproof vest and all you'll feel is a tiny little thud, like maybe a fly bumped into you! That's all! Your bulletproof vest will protect you!

Are you ready to try it? Close your eyes. See yourself with your vest on. Think of one more time in the past when someone gave you a put-down. It could be a put-down from an older person or from someone your own age. Hear the person's words and imagine the put-down coming at you. But then watch that put-down bounce off your vest and fall right to the ground! *Pause.* It doesn't hurt you at

all! *Pause.* **Were you able to imagine it? Do you like the bulletproof vest idea?**

Debrief the experience. Give students an opportunity to tell which images were particularly effective for them. Ask if there are any other images they might use instead. Ask if they can think of times they might use one of these images in the future. You might take a quick, informal vote on which image students liked best.

Would you like to practice a little more as a class? *Pause.* **Everyone stand up. This time the puppet will give a put-down to everyone in the class. I'd like each of you to decide right now which imagination technique you want to use. Remember—when you're imagining, you don't say anything. You'll just imagine the puppet's put-down coming at you like a rock and imagine how you'll keep it from hitting you.**

To make this exercise more fun, I'd like each of you to practice acting out what you're imagining. For instance, if you decide to imagine putting up an invisible shield, you might act like this. *Model in an exaggerated manner putting up a shield.* **Now, you try it with me.** *Encourage students to exaggerate their movements and dramatize putting up a shield.* **Good job! That should stop any put-down.**

Lead students in dramatizing the other scenarios—being a karate expert and jumping aside or giving a karate chop, or having the put-down bounce off their bulletproof vest. Encourage students to really "get into" their movements.

That was fun! Now I'd like you to practice a few more times. Remember, exaggerate your motions as you act out the technique you're imagining; that will help you learn it. Later, when you use this technique with a real put-downer, you'll act out the technique only in your imagination, and no one will know the clever trick you're using. People will just wonder why the put-down didn't work!

Are you ready for the puppet to give you a put-down? Decide what technique you want to imagine and act it out after the puppet hurls its insult. O.K.? *Sample put-downs follow. After each example, take a poll to see how many students used each of the images. Ask if they were able to imagine the put-down missing them.*

- I like your funny hat—oh, sorry, that's your hair!

- Those are great looking pants. Too bad they didn't have your size!

- With feet like yours, who needs skis?

- Where did you get your brains? At the toy store?

- Is that your lunch, or are you taking out the garbage?

- You eat like a pig with hiccups!

- My dog can catch a ball better than you can!

- Why don't you drink some spot remover and disappear?

Summarize by saying: **You're doing a really good job with the imagining technique. If you get a put-down, you can use this imagination trick right after you do the ignoring technique. The wonderful thing about the imagination trick is that no one knows what you're thinking! People only see you looking strong and proud.**

REVIEW OF SKILLS PRESENTED

So, you've now learned two different ways to handle put-downs. Can you tell me what they are? *Allow for student response. When finished, put Transparency #2, "Techniques to Use With Put-Downers," on the overhead.*

Good! We can ignore put-downs and we can use our imaginations to stop them from "getting to us." I'm going to put up this poster in the room to help us remember to use these techniques if we get any put-downs. *(Display Poster #1 of the same title.)*

LESSON REVIEW

Review the lesson by having students respond verbally to one or more of the following sentence stems:

- *I learned . . . .*

- *I was surprised . . . .*

- *I liked . . . .*

- *I didn't like . . . .*

- *A time I'll use what I learned is when . . . .*

STUDENTS TALLY AND GRAPH THEIR OWN PUT-DOWNS AND FRIENDLY COMMENTS

Lesson 1, Handout #1

Have students continue to keep track of any put-downs and positive comments they give, and for a portion of time each day have them tally and graph these comments using Handout #1, "Keeping Count," from Lesson 1. Watching their put-downs decrease and their positive interactions increase is a powerful motivator for behavior change and learning.

SUPPLEMENTARY ACTIVITIES

Use the following Supplementary Activities to reinforce lesson concepts:

- *"The Way I'll Use My Imagination to Protect Myself From Put-Downs"*
  (Supplementary Activity #1)

- *"Using My Imagination to Block Put-Downs"*
  (Supplementary Activity #2)

TRANSPARENCY #1

What to Imagine
When You Get a Put-Down

Imagining one of the following things can help keep put-downs from "sinking in."

invisible shield

karate expert

bulletproof vest

TRANSPARENCY #2/POSTER #1

Techniques to Use With Put-Downers

1. Ignoring

2. Imagination

The Way I'll Use My Imagination to Protect Myself From Put-Downs

Objective   Students will select an imagination technique and practice determining when to use it.

Materials   Supplementary Activity #1 Handout, "The Way I'll Use My Imagination to Protect Myself From Put-Downs"

Scissors

Paste

Markers or crayons

Rulers or flat sticks

Puppet

Procedure   Tell students that in this activity they will make a figure of themselves with a shield, karate outfit, or bulletproof vest and use it to practice determining when to use their favorite imagination technique for protecting themselves from put-downs. Give each student a copy of Supplementary Activity #1 Handout, "The Way I'll Use My Imagination to Protect Myself From Put-Downs." Have students draw hair, facial features, and clothing on the figure at the center of the handout, making it look like them. Next, have them color the protective device of their choice. Then, instruct them to cut out the figure and the device and glue the device onto the figure.

After they have completed their "imagination figures," use a hand puppet to deliver both put-downs and friendly comments to the students, either to the whole class or individually. Students should listen carefully and respond by smiling at the friendly comments or by holding up their imagination figures when they hear a put-down.

Put-downs and friendly comments you might use follow:

- Hey, Brainless!

- Your hair looks nice today.

- Hi-ya, Potato-Face!

- You sure can throw the ball a long way!

- What's up, Beetle-Breath?

- Who picks out your clothes—your little brother?

- Thanks for lending me a pencil.

- The last time I saw someone as funny looking as you, I was at the zoo!

- Do you have a driver's license? You're driving **me** crazy!

- I'd like to sit by you at lunch.

- What a baby! When are you going to grow up?

- Would you like some of my potato chips?

- You eat like you haven't had any food in three weeks!

- Close your mouth; we might fall in!

SUPPLEMENTARY ACTIVITY #1 HANDOUT

The Way I'll Use My Imagination to Protect Myself From Put-Downs

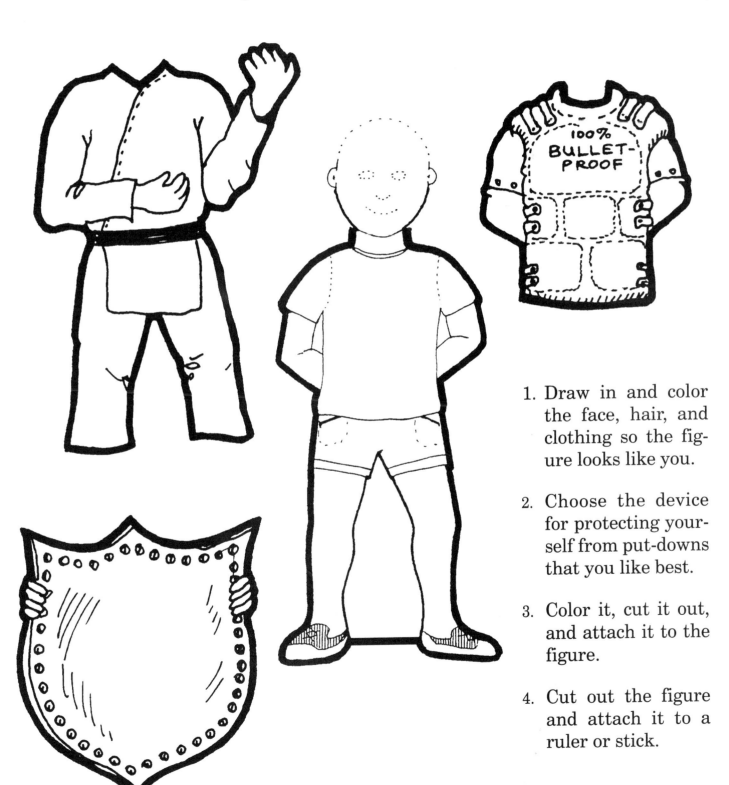

100%
BULLET-
PROOF

1. Draw in and color the face, hair, and clothing so the figure looks like you.

2. Choose the device for protecting yourself from put-downs that you like best.

3. Color it, cut it out, and attach it to the figure.

4. Cut out the figure and attach it to a ruler or stick.

SUPPLEMENTARY ACTIVITY #2

Using My Imagination to Block Put-Downs

Objective   Students will role-play using their imaginations to protect themselves from put-down statements.

Materials   Ball of wadded paper

Supplementary Activity #2 Handout, "I Can Use My Imagination!"

Puppet

Procedure   Review with students the imaginary defenses against put-downs that were taught in the lesson: using an invisible shield, using a karate move, and using a bulletproof vest. Ask for volunteers to play an imagination game with you. Tell the students that you'll use a hand puppet to deliver an insult and toss a wad of paper at each volunteer. The volunteer is to act out one of the imaginary defenses—karate-chopping or side-stepping the paper wad, holding up his or her shield, or jutting out his or her chest while holding in place an imaginary bulletproof vest.

After this practice time, distribute the "I Can Use My Imagination!" handout and instruct students to color the three figures, adding facial features and hair to match their own. Ask them to put a star above the imagination technique that they like the best. These handouts can be taped to students' desks or put inside a folder.

SUPPLEMENTARY ACTIVITY #2 HANDOUT

I Can Use My Imagination!

Draw facial features and hair onto each of the three figures to make them look like you. Then color the figures. Put a star above the figure using the imagination technique that you like the best for protecting yourself from put-downs.

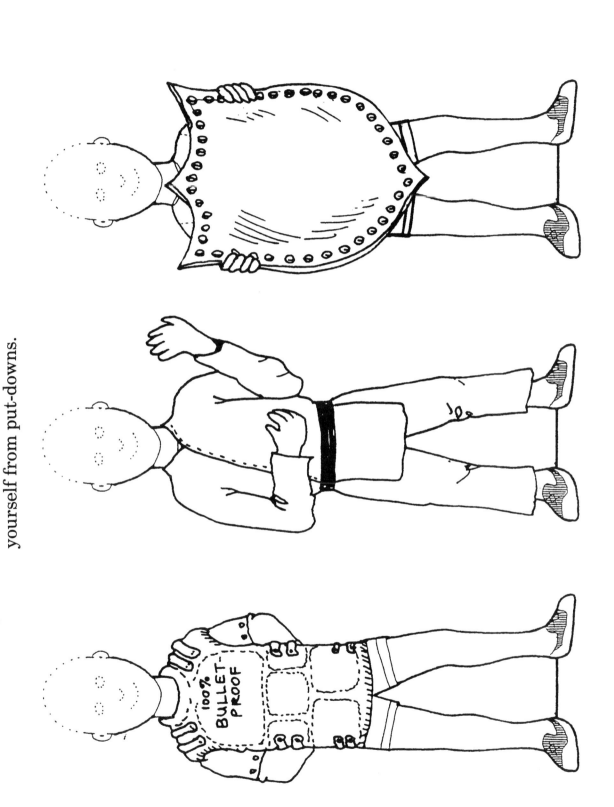

How to Keep Put-Downs From Hurting Self-Esteem: Using Agreeing Responses and "Crazy Compliments"

Objective Students will learn the assertive techniques of agreeing with put-downs and giving "crazy compliments."

Materials Transparency #2 from Lesson 2 – "Techniques to Use With Put-Downers"

Transparency #1 – "Being Clever But Not Mean"

Transparency #2/Handout #1 – "What to Say When You Get a Put-Down: Agree With the Put-Downer"

Teacher Sheet from Lesson 1 – "Insult Bank for Guided Practice"

Transparency #3 – "Give a CRAZY COMPLIMENT"

Transparency #4/Handout #2 – "What to Say When You Get a Put-Down: Give a Crazy Compliment"

Handout #3 – "Pick the Best Comments to These Put-Downs"

Poster – "Caution: No Put-Down Zone"

Handout #1 from Lesson 1 – "Keeping Count"

Puppet

Transparency marker

To the Teacher

This lesson teaches students two more techniques they can use to deflect put-downs without escalating conflict. In the previous lesson they learned to deflect put-downs with nonverbal responses. In this lesson, they will learn how to respond verbally in an assertive but nonaggressive way through the techniques of agreeing with the put-down and of giving a crazy compliment. These two responses usually disarm and surprise the antagonizer. They also have the potential of winning his or her respect, thus leaving the way open for friendship.

It may be difficult for some students to let go of their old patterns of responding to a put-down with another put-down. Should they respond with a put-down during practice sessions, it will be important to label the response as a put-down and to point out that this kind of response is not helpful, since it will almost invariably bring more put-downs in return. It will also be important to point out that this type of response makes the student's behavior just as bad as that of the "put-downer."

You may wish to give the students a copy of Handout #1 ("What to Say When You Get a Put-Down: Agree With the Put-Downer") and Handout #2 ("What to Say When You Get a Put-Down: Give a Crazy Compliment") so they can easily refer to the agreeing and crazy compliment responses during practice sessions. (To save paper, you can copy these handouts back-to-back.) As in the previous lessons, be sure to use a puppet when giving put-downs.

Keep in mind that the skills taught in this lesson will require a great deal of practice and reinforcement before becoming second nature to most students.

If you have students use Handout #1 from Lesson 1 ("Keeping Count") as suggested at the end of this lesson, draw their attention to the tally marks they have made in each column. Encourage them to make an effort during the weeks ahead to decrease the number of put-downs they give and increase the number of friendly comments. Help them to do so by predicting that by week three there will probably be very few tallies in the "Put-Down" column and lots of tallies in the "Friendly Comments" column since they will all be reminding one another to be kind rather than critical.

Lesson Presentation

REVIEW OF THE IGNORING AND IMAGINATION TECHNIQUES

Lesson 2, Transp. #2

In our last lesson we talked about some effective ways to deal with put-downs. The techniques you learned will help you feel confident and better able to protect yourselves when someone says something mean to you. Who can remember what those techniques were? *Allow for student response. Put Transparency #2 from Lesson 2, "Techniques to Use With Put-Downers," on the overhead and review the techniques of ignoring the put-down and using the imagination to deflect put-downs.*

SOMETIMES WE NEED TO RESPOND TO A PUT-DOWN

Although these tricks are very powerful and helpful, once in a while you'll want to say something back to a kid who is putting you down.

When responding to a put-down, most kids say something mean to the put-downer. They feel hurt and angry, and they want to hurt back. Their response may make them feel better for the moment, but in the long run it does more harm than good. For one thing, it will usually cause them to get more put-downs in return, putting them right back where they started from! Plus, it turns them into a

put-downer themselves; they have acted just as badly as the person who put them down.

Transp. #1

It's much better to surprise the put-downer with a comment that's cool and clever but not mean. *Put Transparency #1, "Being Clever But Not Mean," on the overhead.* **Here's a girl who is learning to be clever but not mean when she says something back to a put-downer. Someone has just given her a put-down.** *Read the put-down statement inside the top arrow.* **She is thinking of several things she could say back.** *Point out these responses on the transparency and read them aloud.*

One of these comments is mean. Which one is it? *Allow students to tell which response is a put-down.* **Right! But this girl doesn't like put-downs, so she doesn't want to say something that will make her a put-downer herself. She decides to choose one of the clever comments instead. Let's vote and see which one you think she should choose.**

Read the statements again, allowing students to vote on the ones that are their favorites. Circle the statement that is the class's first choice. **Good choice. Let's read the put-down and response again and see how the response sounds.** *Read the put-down again, and then the chosen response. (You may want to let the class say the response aloud.) Then review the other put-downs and responses on the transparency in the same manner, encouraging students to distinguish between put-down responses and clever retorts.*

Good job! It's a lot more fun to say something clever and surprising to the put-downer, than to say something mean. *(Since a handout similar to this transparency will be used for reinforcement at the end of the lesson, it's best to remove this transparency now and not use it again when teaching the following techniques.)*

AGREEING WITH THE PUT-DOWNER

There are two kinds of clever comments you can use when you want to say something back to a put-downer. In fact, both types were represented on the transparency we just looked at. The first type of clever comment is—believe it or not—to AGREE with the put-downer! I know that sounds weird, but you'll be amazed at how well it works!

Transp. #2

Put Transparency #2, "What to Say When You Get a Put-Down: Agree With the Put-Downer," on the overhead, exposing only the cartoon at the bottom. Read and discuss the cartoon, describing what may have happened to lead up to the scene shown here. Then ask: **How do you think this put-downer felt when the other boy didn't get mad or upset as a result of the put-down? Do you think the put-downer got what he wanted?** *Allow for student response.*

Agreeing with put-downers takes them by surprise, and they often can't think of what to say next. By "agreeing," I don't mean you REALLY agree with the put-downer; what I mean is that you say something clever that shows you refuse to let the put-downer get to you—that you refuse to get upset and give a put-down back. Your response will show that you're cool, calm, and confident.

I have a list of agreeing responses you can use when a put-downer tries to make you mad. Let's look at the list and see which ones are your favorites. *Read the list on the transparency to the students, uncovering one response at a time. You may wish to let students vote for their two favorite responses, tallying their votes beside the numerals. Add any other agreeing comments students can think of at the bottom of the list.*

**Puppet
Handout #1**

Let's practice this agreeing technique. *Bring out your hand puppet.* **This puppet is in a really grouchy mood today. He's** *(or she's)* **been snapping at everyone since school started. He** *(she)* **wants everyone else to be in a bad mood, too. See if you can surprise him** *(her)* **by using the agreeing technique whenever he** *(she)* **throws a put-down at you.** *Give students a copy of Handout #1, "What to Say When You Get a Put-Down: Agree With the Put-Downer," so they can refer to it during this practice session. Students may want to underline their favorite comments.*

**Lesson 1,
Teacher Sheet**

Using the puppet, move quickly around the room delivering put-downs to students. You can use examples from the Teacher Sheet from Lesson 1 ("Insult Bank for Guided Practice") if you like. Encourage students to hold their heads high and use a strong, but pleasant, voice when they deliver their favorite agreeing statements.

When you feel that the students are comfortable using the technique, say or paraphrase: **You did very well at that! How do you think this puppet put-downer felt when he** *(she)* **couldn't put you in a bad mood? Did** he *(she)* get what he *(she)* wanted? How did it feel to stand up to him *(her)*? Did you feel strong? Did you feel in charge? Can you think of some times this technique could work for you? *Allow for student response.*

HANDLING A PUT-DOWN THAT THE STUDENT THINKS IS PARTLY TRUE

Once in a while you may think that a put-down that someone gives you has some truth to it, even though you know that most of the put-down is just the put-downer's opinion or an exaggeration. Agreeing is still a powerful response, and a good way to get the other person to stop insulting you.

In such instances, you can keep the put-down from hurting by imagining that you're wearing a bulletproof vest, so that the put-down doesn't sink in. Never let yourself spend time feeling bad about what the person said. Instead, think of things you like about yourself—things you do well.

GIVING A "CRAZY COMPLIMENT"

Transp. #3

I have another trick I think you'll like. This one can be great fun, and you can really use your imagination. *Put Transparency #3, "Give a CRAZY COMPLIMENT," on the overhead, covering all but the first frame.* This technique really bugs put-downers because it shows them you aren't bothered by their put-downs. You give them a "crazy compliment"! They will be so surprised by your crazy compliment, they may think you didn't even notice the put-down! *Read and explain the first frame, asking questions like the following:* How do you think the put-downer felt when the boy told her she had great eyebrows? Do you think that was the kind of response she expected? Does the boy she put down look upset, or does he look calm and confident? *Read and discuss the remaining three frames in the same way.*

Giving put-downers a crazy compliment really takes them by surprise, doesn't it? When you give them a crazy compliment, they know their put-down didn't get to you.

A LIST OF CRAZY COMPLIMENTS

Put Transparency #4, "What to Say When You Get a Put-Down: Give a Crazy Compliment," on the overhead, covering up all but the first response. **Here's a list of crazy compliments you can use to surprise put-downers. Let's read the crazy compliments and see which ones you like the best.** *Uncover the crazy compliments one at a time and read them to the students, adding student suggestions at the bottom of the transparency. Have students vote for their two favorites. Tally the votes next to each crazy compliment.*

Let's practice giving some crazy compliments. *Give students copies of Handout #2, "What to Say When You Get a Put-Down: Give a Crazy Compliment," so they can refer to the responses.* **This puppet is going to give you some put-downs, and I want you to raise your hand if you want to give him** *(her)* **a crazy compliment in response. You may use one of the crazy compliments from the list or make up your own.** *Have the puppet give the following four put-downs or four put-downs you've made up, one at a time, and have students raise their hands to give their crazy compliments:*

- **You look like an octopus when you jump rope!**

- **Your story was so boring I almost fell asleep.**

- **Nice poster! I didn't know you could draw with your toes!**

- **Your feet are so big I'll bet you don't even need swim fins when you go to the pool!**

After the practice session, say or paraphrase: **Great! Isn't that a fun technique? And it's a pretty easy one to use, too. Try it the next time you get a put-down and tell me what happens.**

STUDENTS PRACTICE USING BOTH TECHNIQUES

When you respond to a put-down by giving a crazy compliment or by agreeing with it, you'll find that you really impress other kids. Everyone likes a kid who has a good sense of humor and can joke about things—even put-downs! And everyone respects kids who can keep their cool and not blow up.

Let's play a put-down game. My puppet will give a put-down. Then I'll call on a volunteer to say something back. The volunteer should

either agree with the put-down or respond with a crazy compliment. Everyone else should listen closely and decide which technique the volunteer used. If you think you know, hold up your hand. *Use your puppet to deliver the following put-downs (or others selected from the "Insult Bank for Guided Practice"). Choose student volunteers to respond to the put-downs and call on other students to identify the kind of responses the volunteers used (either agreeing or crazy compliment).*

- **Would you like me to ask a kindergartner to help you with your spelling?**

- **You can't play with us; dorks aren't allowed in this game.**

- **I can't believe you couldn't work that problem! It was the easiest one on the test!**

- **What a cute little monkey! Oh, sorry, I didn't recognize you!**

- **Don't you ever comb your hair?**

- **You've worn that same outfit every day.**

- **My cat can write neater than you!**

If a student volunteer offers a response that is a put-down rather than a crazy compliment or an agreeing comment, say something like, "We can't use that, because it's a put-down. Why don't we want to give a put-down back? Right, because we'd be as bad as the put-downer and we'd just get more put-downs in return!"

LESSON REVIEW

Handout #3

Have students complete Handout #3, "Pick the Best Comments to These Put-Downs," and review their responses to assess their understanding of the lesson. Further discuss any problem areas.

Then review the lesson by having students respond verbally to one or more of the following sentence stems:

- *I learned . . . .*

- *I was surprised . . . .*

- *I liked . . . .*

- *I wish . . . .*

Poster

You may want to hang the poster "Caution: No Put-Down Zone" as a visual reminder to students to keep the classroom free from put-downs.

BEING ALERT AND PREPARED FOR PUT-DOWNS

Lesson 1, Handout #1

We've talked about why kids usually give put-downs—because they want to make other kids laugh, so that they'll be more popular, or because they want to see someone get upset. And we've practiced several different ways to respond to put-downs that will make a put-down not work. Since we're all alert and prepared for put-downs, we'll probably have fewer put-downs in our class this week than last. Let's keep counting, just the same, using our charts as we did before. *Have students tally and graph their use of put-downs and friendly comments to facilitate the transfer of training.*

Also, if you hear someone give someone a put-down, be sure to say to them, "That's a put-down." If you should get a put-down from a kid outside of our classroom, I hope you'll remember to either ignore it or use the agreeing or crazy compliment techniques you learned today.

SUPPLEMENTARY ACTIVITIES

Use the grade-leveled Supplementary Activities that follow this lesson to reinforce lesson concepts:

- *2nd Grade*

"They Say—You Say"
   (Supplementary Activity #1)

"Surprise Them With a Comment That Shows You're Cool and Clever"
   (Supplementary Activity #2)

- *3rd Grade*

"Practice in Agreeing With Put-Downs and Giving Crazy Compliments"
   (Supplementary Activity #3)

"No Matter How You Feel About a Put-Down, Be Calm, Cool, and Clever"
   (Supplementary Activity #4)

TRANSPARENCY #1

Being Clever But Not Mean

Your hair looks like the dog slept on it!

> Bug off, Banana-Nose.
> Disgusting, isn't it?
> Amazing, but true.
> That's an interesting way to look at it.

You're such a bad player, nobody wants you on their team.

> Stop! You're breaking my heart.
> Watch it or I'll call my lawyer.
> Would you put that in writing?
> You're the rotten player, Klutz!

Don't you EVER wear anything new?

> I try not to. Thanks for noticing.
> Drop dead, Geek!
> Hard to believe, isn't it?
> Thanks for the compliment.

TRANSPARENCY #2/HANDOUT #1

What to Say
When You Get a Put Down:
Agree With the Put-Downer

_____ 1. Amazing, but true.

_____ 2. Hard to believe, isn't it?

_____ 3. Nice of you to notice.

_____ 4. That's an interesting way to look at it.

_____ 5. Yep, that's me all over.

_____ 6. Yeah, wasn't that a great mistake!

_____ 7. That was supposed to be a secret!

_____ 8. Cool, huh!

_____ 9. That's life!

_____ 10. Whatever.

Your ideas:

_____

_____

_____

_____

TRANSPARENCY #3

Give a CRAZY COMPLIMENT

TRANSPARENCY #4/HANDOUT #2

What to Say
When You Get a Put-Down:
Give a Crazy Compliment

_____ 1. Nice eyebrows!

_____ 2. Nice nostrils!

_____ 3. Nice ears!

_____ 4. Nice shoelaces!

_____ 5. Nice elbows!

_____ 6. Nice eyelids!

_____ 7. Nice tonsils!

_____ 8. Nice arms—your left one's even better than your right!

_____ 9. Your ideas:

_____

_____

> Nice eyebrows!

HANDOUT #3

Pick the Best Comments to These Put-Downs

1. **Draw a line** through the comments that are mean.
2. **Circle** the crazy compliments.
3. **Put a star** in front of the agreeing comments.

Your hair looks like the dog slept on it!

> Bug off, Banana-Nose.
> Amazing, but true.
> That's an interesting way to look at it.
> Nice nostrils!

You're such a bad player, nobody wants you on their team.

> Nice eyebrows!
> You've got a great set of tonsils!
> That was supposed to be a secret.
> You're the rotton player, Klutz!

Don't you EVER wear anything new?

> I try not to. Thanks for noticing.
> Drop dead, Geek!
> Hard to believe, isn't it?
> I like your eyelids!

Write one of your own:

POSTER

They Say—You Say

What is this mean kid saying?

What could this boy say back that wouldn't be another put-down? Imagine that he'll use the agreeing trick or the crazy compliment trick.

Imagine that these kids are putting you down. What are they saying?

What could you say back that would be powerful but wouldn't be a put-down?

SUPPLEMENTARY ACTIVITY #2

Surprise Them With a Comment That Shows You're Cool and Clever

When they say:

You could say:

SUPPLEMENTARY ACTIVITY #3

Practice Agreeing With Put-Downs and Giving Crazy Compliments

Objective   Students will practice responding to put-downs with the techniques of giving a crazy compliment and agreeing with the put-downs.

Materials   Supplementary Activity #3 Handout, "Put-Down Cards (3rd Grade)" (cut cards apart and put them in a small box or basket)

Class poster made from Transparency #2 from the lesson, "What to Say When You Get a Put-Down: Agree With the Put-Downer" (optional)

Class poster made from Transparency #4 from the lesson, "What to Say When You Get a Put-Down: Give a Crazy Compliment" (optional)

Box or basket for cards

Puppet

Procedure   In this activity students gain practical experience to increase their facility in using agreeing responses and giving crazy compliments to put-downs.

Explain to the students that in this exercise they will role-play responding to put-downs with agreeing responses or crazy compliments. Select two student volunteers. Have one of the volunteers randomly pick a Put-Down Card from the box or basket but not read it.

Explain that you'll have your puppet read the put-down situation aloud and then you'll give the volunteers a moment to think of a good crazy compliment or agreeing response. The first volunteer should give his or her response and class members should put their thumbs up if they think the response would work with the put-down. Next, the second volunteer should give his or her response, and the class as a whole should repeat the "thumbs-up" assessment.

After the first two volunteers have had their turn, ask for a new set of student volunteers and continue with the role-plays. If both volunteers respond by using the same technique (either a crazy compliment or an agreeing response), you may wish to ask the other class members to suggest an appropriate response using the other technique.

Continue until you feel the class has had adequate practice.

SUPPLEMENTARY ACTIVITY #3 HANDOUT

Put-Down Cards (3rd Grade)

While you are waiting at your bus stop, a group of kids comes by. One of the kids starts to call you names.	You just got a new pair of athletic shoes. You really like them. When you walk into class a kid shouts, "Ha! Those shoes were really popular—LAST YEAR!"
You're at recess playing with your friends. A bully comes up and says, "You're dressed a little early for Halloween!"	You ask your teacher to read the class a book you think is great. When your teacher does, some of the kids tell you they thought it was a dumb book.
You missed half of the words on the spelling test. The kid in front of you tells his neighbor you're stupid.	You're doing an art project. Another kid says, "What a mess; you're just wasting paper."
You were given a game as a birthday present. You bring it to school to show your friends, but they all tease you about it and say it's for little kids.	You're on the school bus. All the kids start chanting that you're a nerd.
Some kids are playing ball. You ask if you can play. One says, "I don't want to play with a klutz."	There are a few math facts you just can't seem to remember. Every time the class plays a math game, you miss some. A couple of kids have started calling you "The Math Wizard."

SUPPLEMENTARY ACTIVITY #4

No Matter How You Feel About a Put-Down, Be Calm, Cool, and Clever

1. How do you **feel** when you get a put-down?
   Check the responses that are true for you.

   _____ a. Hurt

   _____ b. Dumb

   _____ c. Like no one likes me

   _____ d. Angry

   _____ e. Embarrassed

   _____ f. Like a bad person

2. What do you feel like **doing** when you get a put-down?
   Check the responses that are true for you.

   _____ a. Saying something mean to the put-downer

   _____ b. Crying

   _____ c. Getting someone else to help you

   _____ d. Beating up on the person

   _____ e. Trying to get the put-downer to like you

   _____ f. Getting away from the whole situation

   _____ g. Tattling on the put-downer

   _____ h. Taking the hurt you feel out on someone else

3. What could you do when you get a put-down that would surprise the put-downer and make you look calm, cool, and clever?

   _____

   _____

   _____

How to Keep Put-Downs From Hurting Self-Esteem: Using Self-Encouragement

Objective   Students will learn to encourage themselves with positive self-talk when they have been given a put-down.

Students will learn to encourage friends who have been put down by others.

Materials   Transparency #1 – "Things You Can Say to Make Yourself Feel Better"

Transparency #2/Handout #1 – "What to Say to Yourself to Keep Put-Downs From Hurting"

Transparency #3 – "Sometimes We Give Ourselves a Put-Down"

Transparency #4 – "Which Is Better to Say to Yourself?"

Transparency #5/Handout #2 – "How to Be a Friend to Someone Who Has Been Put Down"

Poster #2 from Lesson 1 – "Keeping Count"
   or

Handout #1 from Lesson 1 – "Keeping Count"

Puppet

Poster from Lesson 3 – "Caution: No Put-Down Zone" (optional)

Transparency marker

To the Teacher

It is an almost automatic reaction for children to respond defensively when they receive a disparaging remark or to silently agree with the attacker and feel badly about themselves. Thus far, the lessons in this module have taught students to counter those reactions by ignoring put-downs, using their imagination, and using the verbal skills of agreeing with the put-downer or responding with a crazy compliment.

In this lesson, students will learn that even the best skills and techniques can't always prevent put-downs from "getting to them"—either hurting them or making them mad. They'll be reminded that they may, at times, agree with the put-downer and in such instances may give themselves additional put-downs or negative self-assessments, making themselves feel even worse.

However, students can make an effort to prevent this from happening. They will learn that they can make themselves feel better when they have been hurt by a put-down by thinking things about themselves that are self-affirming as well as **true**. (Although statements that are exaggeratedly flattering may appear comforting, they don't really help a wounded ego. A child's sense of integrity won't allow him or her to believe something that isn't true.)

Students will also learn that this skill of saying something kind can be a friendship tool. They can use it to help someone else feel better after that person has been put down by another. They will practice this skill with their Learning Partners.

If your students have been using either Poster #2 or Handout #1 from Lesson 1 ("Keeping Count"), have them continue to tally the put-downs and friendly comments they hear. Draw their attention, again, to the number of tallies in each column and discuss their implications.

You may wish to hang up the poster from Lesson 3, "Caution: No Put-Down Zone," if you have not already done so.

Lesson Presentation

REVIEW OF PREVIOUS LESSONS

Puppet

You've been practicing some ways of dealing with put-downers without being mean. One of the techniques you've been practicing is ignoring the put-down. Will someone volunteer to give us a demonstration of this technique? My puppet will deliver the put-down. *Use a puppet to give the student volunteer a put-down. Guide the student through the ignoring technique.*

Good job! Now I need some of you to act out the imagining technique. *Continue using the puppet, and choose student volunteers to demonstrate the three imagination techniques: using a shield, using karate moves, and wearing a bulletproof vest. Ask the class to identify each technique used.* **Good! Our imaginations can help us keep put-downs from hurting us.**

You've also learned how to say something clever but not mean in response to a put-down. Will someone volunteer to show us the technique of agreeing with the put-downer? *Use the puppet to deliver a put-down, and have a student volunteer agree with the put-down.* **Great! Now can someone volunteer to show us the technique of giving a crazy compliment in response to a put-down?** *Choose another student volunteer to demonstrate giving a crazy compliment in response to a put-down delivered by the puppet.* **Thank you for helping! I'm glad to see that you are remembering these new ways of dealing with a put-downer.**

SAYING HELPFUL THINGS TO YOURSELF

Even though all of these techniques can help protect us from put-downs, once in a while someone will say something mean that takes us totally by surprise. A put-down can sneak up on us before we have a chance to defend ourselves from it. And it hurts! When that happens, we need to find a way to make ourselves feel better.

Let's talk for a minute about what you do when you get hurt when you're playing. How many of you have ever fallen when you were playing and scraped your knee? *Allow for a show of hands.* **If you fall and scrape your knee and your knee is all dirty and bleeding, you need to take care of it. What are some things that could make your hurt knee feel better?** *Have students share what makes them feel better when they're hurt. Typical responses are: having a parent clean and bandage the wound; getting a hug; washing and bandaging the wound themselves; and having a friend notice the wound and sympathize. Summarize by saying:* **You can see that there are many different ways to make yourself feel better when you get physically hurt.**

When someone says something mean to you and it makes you hurt on the inside, you need to take care of that hurt, too. Just as you might put medicine or a bandage on a scraped knee to make it feel better, you can say kind things to yourself to make yourself feel better when you've been put down.

TO BE HELPFUL, SELF-STATEMENTS HAVE TO BE TRUE

Transp. #1

I'm not talking about saying things to yourself like, "I'm the BEST kid in the school!" or "EVERYBODY in the whole world wants to be my friend!" I'm talking about kind statements that are also <u>true</u> statements—those are the only ones that really make you feel better. Today you'll learn some of those statements. *Put Transparency #1, "Things You Can Say to Make Yourself Feel Better," on the overhead.*

You might say to yourself, "I'm still a good person" *(point to this bubble on the transparency),* **or you might remind yourself, "Other people like me"** *(point to this bubble on the transparency).* **Can you think of other kind things you could say to yourself when someone has hurt you with a**

put-down? *Lead students in brainstorming true, positive self-statements. Write two of these in the other bubbles on the transparency.*

EXAMPLES OF HELPFUL SELF-STATEMENTS

Transp. #2

Here are some other helpful comments kids have used to make themselves feel better when people have given them put-downs. Let's see which ones you like the best. *Show students Transparency #2, "What to Say to Yourself to Keep Put-Downs From Hurting," and read through the list of self-statements. Use the two blank lines to add to the list the two statements you added to the bubbles on Transparency #1. You may want to have students vote on their favorites.*

Handout #1

I'm going to give you a copy of this list so you can practice saying kind things to yourself when you get a put-down. I encourage you to look at the list whenever you need to, even after we've finished this lesson. Saying something kind to yourself really can take the sting out of a put-down. *Distribute Handout #1, "What to Say to Yourself to Keep Put-Downs From Hurting." Students may wish to put a star by their favorite statements.*

PRACTICING MAKING HELPFUL SELF-STATEMENTS

Saying kind things to yourself is hard to practice because it all happens on the inside. So, let's do this—I'll have my puppet give put-downs to the whole class. When you hear each put-down, think of something nice to say to yourself. You can choose one of the statements on your handout or you can make up a kind statement of your own. What's important is that you think of something to say to yourself that would make you feel better if my puppet hurt your feelings or made you mad.

Now, let's try it. *Use the puppet to give the following put-downs to the class as a whole. (Note that these put-downs are less humorous than previous examples, so that students can identify a little more readily with a feeling of hurt or anger.) After each put-down, wait a moment and then call on a student volunteer to say aloud the kind statement he or she might use. Compliment students on their ability to be a good friend to themselves when a put-downer "gets to them."*

- **Nice clothes! Did you make them yourself?**

- **What a loser you are!**

- **Nice move, Clumsy!**

- **Nobody can read your handwriting, it's so messy.**

- **If I had a face like yours, I'd walk backwards!**

- **What a dumb looking art project!**

- **You couldn't hit a baseball if it was sitting still!**

- **We don't want you in our club.**

- **My pet turtle can go faster than you.**

After delivering a few put-downs in this manner, you may want to move swiftly around the room using the puppet to give put-downs to individual students. Have students say aloud what they would say to themselves to feel better. Leave Transparency #2 on the overhead so students can refer to it during this exercise.

SUGGESTIONS FOR REINFORCING THE USE OF HELPFUL SELF-STATEMENTS

Since the process being practiced is an internal one, it can be difficult to determine whether students are learning and using it. Here are some suggestions for reinforcing the use of positive self-statements when students receive put-downs. (1) Have the students write their favorite positive self-statements on a slip of paper and keep these in their supply boxes or folders; (2) Hang up a poster containing a list of short, positive self-statements for student reference and then use your puppet to deliver put-downs several times during the next week so students can practice this "self-encouragement" exercise; (3) Since a tangible reminder is often comforting to children, have students write their favorite positive self-statement on a small card and keep it in their pocket. If someone puts them down, they can reach into their pocket and touch the card as they remind themselves of what it says.

SOMETIMES WE GIVE OURSELVES PUT-DOWNS

`Transp. #3` **Sometimes, when someone gives us a put-down, we may agree with the put-downer. We forget that others don't know the whole truth** about us and that they don't know about all of our good points. We think their opinion of us must be true, and so in our minds we agree with the put-down. *Place Transparency #3, "Sometimes We Give Ourselves a Put-Down," on the overhead.*

Listen to this story and see if something like this has ever happened to you:

> Alex's baseball team was having its turn to be in the field. Although Alex was a pretty good batter, he wasn't the greatest at catching the ball. When the batter for the other team hit a ball right toward him, Alex dropped it and the other team scored a run! Someone behind Alex yelled, "Give it up, Alex! You'll never be any good!" Alex thought to himself, "He's right—I'm a rotten player."

Poor Alex! How many of you have had an experience like that? *Ask students to raise their thumbs if they've had something similar happen to them.* Did you notice that Alex got <u>two</u> put-downs? Who gave Alex the first put-down? *Allow for student response.*

Yes, Alex's teammate put him down for dropping the ball. That was the first put-down. But who gave Alex the second put-down? *Allow for student response. Students should observe that Alex put himself down as a bad ballplayer.*

Alex made himself feel WORSE by believing the put-downer. He gave himself another put-down in his mind! How many of you know what that's like? *Have students raise their thumbs if they do. Ask the students if any of them would be willing to share a story about a time when they gave themselves a put-down. You might model a self-put-down of your own.* Just because someone says something unkind to us, that doesn't mean that it's true. There's no reason to make ourselves feel worse by giving ourselves another put-down.

PRACTICING CHOOSING POSITIVE SELF-STATEMENTS
RATHER THAN SELF-PUT-DOWNS

Transp. #4

Put Transparency #4, "Which Is Better to Say to Yourself?" on the overhead, covering all but the first example. **I'm going to read you some more** put-downs and some things people might say to themselves in response. Think about which of the self-statements would make the person feel better and which would make the person feel worse. *Read the first put-down.*

Here are some of the things the girl on the right might say to herself. Some of them could make her feel better, and some of them are self-put-downs. Let's cross out the ones that could make her feel worse. *Read the self-statements and allow students to identify them as helpful or unhelpful self-talk. Cross out the negative comments. Continue this process with the remaining four examples. Conclude by saying:* I'm glad to see that you can tell the difference between self-statements that would make you feel better and ones that would make you feel worse.

Remembering to say something to make yourself feel better can be a very tricky thing. Sometimes you won't even <u>know</u> that you believed the put-downer—all you'll notice is that you feel badly. So the best thing to do if you get a put-down is to say something to yourself <u>right away</u> that will make you feel better! Don't wait for even a minute!

WE CAN HELP FRIENDS WHEN THEY GET A PUT-DOWN

Sometimes a friend of yours will get a put-down. How many of you have heard someone say something mean to one of your friends or noticed that a friend of yours was feeling really badly because he or she got a put-down? *Suggest that students raise their thumbs if they have.*

Transp. #5

We can help another person in the same way we just practiced helping ourselves. We can say kind things to another person just the same way we can say kind things to ourselves. *Put Transparency #5, "How to Be a Friend to Someone Who Has Been Put Down," on the overhead. Cover the transparency with two strips of paper so that only the two girls are showing.*

Here are two girls. One of them has just gotten a put-down and the other is saying kind things to help her feel better. Which one got the put-down? Which one is helping? *Allow for student response.* Can someone make up a story about what happened? *Encourage students to volunteer to describe a possible scenario to the class.*

Well, that would certainly make someone feel badly, wouldn't it? *Remove the paper strip covering the statements on the right side of the transparency.* **Here are some things the dark-haired girl might be saying to make her friend feel better.** *Read the statements. Ask students if they have any other ideas and write their ideas at the bottom of the list. Have students vote on the statement they like best. Write this statement in the bubble above the girl's head.*

Next, show the picture of the two boys. Lead the class through the same exercise of making up a scenario and choosing a kind statement to write in the bubble.

ROLE-PLAYING HELPING A FRIEND WHO HAS BEEN PUT DOWN

When someone has given you a put-down, it's nice to have a friend help you feel better. I'd like everyone to get together with your Learning Partners. I'll give each of you a copy of the kind statements we just went over. I want you to use one of them or make one up on your own to help your Learning Partner feel better when my put-down puppet says something mean to him or her.

| Handout #2 |

Distribute copies of Handout #2, "How to Be a Friend to Someone Who Has Been Put Down." Review the comments once again and have students write their two favorites in the bubbles. They may wish to think of helpful comments of their own and write them on their handouts as well.

Select a pair of Learning Partners to model the following activity and coach them through it: Have the students decide who will receive the put-down and who will be the helping friend. Instruct the student who will receive the put-down to look up at the puppet while it "says" the mean comment and then to hang his or her head as if feeling dejected. The helping student should ask what's wrong and then say a helping statement to the dejected student.

After the two students model the activity, ask for two new volunteers. Repeat the activity until you feel students have become adept at responding with helpful comments. Then have all of the pairs of Learning Partners practice. It's probably easiest to deliver the put-downs to all the pairs at once. After each role-play, Learning Partners should switch roles.

You may make up put-downs of your own or use some of the following:

- **That's a dumb looking jacket! Why don't you get a new one?**

- **I'd rather eat a bug than play with you!**

- **Nobody wears jeans like <u>that</u> anymore!**

- **I don't know why you're working so hard on that ugly drawing!**

- **You're so dumb you need to take lessons from a squirrel.**

LESSON REVIEW

Review the lesson by having students respond verbally to one or more of the following sentence stems:

- *I learned . . . .*

- *I was surprised . . . .*

- *I liked . . . .*

- *I'll remember . . . .*

- *A time I'll use what I learned is when . . . .*

BEING ALERT AND PREPARED FOR PUT-DOWNS

**Lesson 1,
Poster #2
or
Lesson 1,
Handout #1**

Refer students to Poster #2 or Handout #1 from Lesson 1, "Keeping Count." **We're going to continue keeping count of the friendly and unfriendly comments we hear in our classroom. I'll bet that this week you'll hear hardly any put-downs. I hope you'll hear lots of friendly comments. I also hope you'll be practicing making yourself feel better by saying positive things to yourself if you do get a put-down. And remember, you can be a <u>really good friend</u> to someone else who has been put down by saying something to help him or her feel better.**

During the next few days, you can help students remember to practice using positive self-talk to neutralize the hurt of a put-down by asking them to share instances when they applied the skill. You may ask them to share with you individually from time to time or to share their experiences in writing.

SUPPLEMENTARY ACTIVITIES

Use the grade-leveled Supplementary Activities that follow this lesson to reinforce lesson concepts:

- *K-1st Grade*

"Would You Feel Good or Feel Bad?"
    (Supplementary Activity #1)

"What to Say If an Adult Puts You Down"
    (Supplementary Activity #2)

- *2nd Grade*

"Don't Give Yourself Put-Downs!"
    (Supplementary Activity #3)

"Cancel Out That Put-Down!"
    (Supplementary Activity #4)

"Does What I Say to Myself Make Me Happy or Sad?"
    (Supplementary Activity #5)

- *3rd Grade*

"Say Kind Things to Yourself When You Get a Put-Down"
    (Supplementary Activity #6)

"Use Kind Words to Help Yourself or a Friend"
    (Supplementary Activity #7)

TRANSPARENCY #1

Things You Can Say to Make Yourself Feel Better

TRANSPARENCY #2/HANDOUT #1

What to Say to Yourself to Keep Put-Downs From Hurting

1. I know I'm a neat kid.

2. Other people like me.

3. They don't know what I'm really like.

4. No matter what they say, I know I'm O.K.

5. I'm not going to let this bother me.

6. I know I'm an O.K. person.

7. They only see me on the outside.

8. So what if **I can't** make them stop. **They can't** get me upset.

9. *Your ideas:*

_____

_____

TRANSPARENCY #3

Sometimes We Give Ourselves a Put-Down

TRANSPARENCY #4

Which Is Better to Say to Yourself?

PUT-DOWN	SELF-STATEMENT

1 You klutz! My dog can catch better than you!

> I'm a rotton player.
> Nobody's perfect.
> That's just one side of me.
> I can't do anything right.

2 Hey, Lizard-Lips! You even scare monsters.

> That kid doesn't know the real me.
> I'm so ugly.
> He's just trying to impress the other kids.
> I like who I am.

3 You **never** get it right, Beetle-Brain.

> He's trying to act cool.
> I'm so dumb.
> I'm probably going to flunk.
> I won't let this bother me. I know I'm O.K.

4 Nice outfit. Did you get it at the thrift store?

> He only sees me on the outside.
> He's just trying to get a laugh from the other kids.
> I look weird in these clothes.

5 Hey, Garbage-Mouth! Nobody wants to sit with **you** at lunch.

> I eat too much.
> Nobody likes me.
> Other kids like me.
> He obviously doesn't know a neat person when he sees one.

TRANSPARENCY #5/HANDOUT#2

How to Be a Friend to Someone Who Has Been Put Down

Pick your two favorite comments and write one in each bubble.

- **Are you O.K.?**

- **Don't pay any attention to them.**

- **What they said isn't true.**

- **They're just showing off.**

- **I think you're neat.**

- **Don't worry—I'm still your friend.**

- **Come on, let's go someplace else.**

- **Just ignore them and come and play with me.**

_____

_____

(your ideas)

SUPPLEMENTARY ACTIVITY #1

Would You Feel Good or Feel Bad?

Draw in a **happy** face if the thought in the balloon would make you **feel good**.
Draw in a **sad** face if the thought in the balloon would make you **feel bad**.
Then add hair and color the pictures.

What to Say If an Adult Puts You Down

Objective   Students will learn appropriate responses to put-downs given by adults and will brainstorm ways to encourage themselves with positive self-talk.

Materials   Supplementary Activity #2 Transparency, "What to Say If an Adult Gives You a Put-Down"

Procedure   Tell students that in this activity they'll be learning what they can do if an adult says something to them that is a put-down. Explain that very few adults will tolerate children responding to them with put-downs. Adults also are unlikely to accept a joking response or an agreeing remark that doesn't sound sincere. The wisest response for a child is usually to remain silent and do what he or she is told.

Tell students that there **may** be times, however, when they can respond to an adult's put-down, if they do so in a way that isn't rude. If they feel the need to respond, saying one of the following statements (or a variation of it) will usually be effective:

- "I'm sorry."

- "I'm trying to do better."

- "I feel bad when you say things like that."

Explain to students that whether or not they feel the need to make a response, they can **always** help themselves feel better when they've been put down by telling themselves an encouraging self-statement. Three encouraging things they might say are:

- "I'm not bad, I'm young."

- "My behavior isn't always good, but **I'm** good."

- "Little by little, I **am** improving."

Show students Supplementary Activity #2 Transparency, "What to Say If an Adult Gives You a Put-Down." Then read aloud the following scenarios, which correspond to the illustrations on the transparency, or make up appropriate scenarios of your own. For each scenario, ask students which of the top statements they think would be good to say and which of the bottom ones would be good to think to themselves. To assist them in understanding how to fit a response to a situation, it may be helpful to comment on why a particular statement might be appropriate or inappropriate.

Scenarios:

- This woman is the boy's neighbor. She's yelling at him for leaving her gate open, because her dog got out of her yard. She's saying that he's "brainless" and "can't be trusted to do anything right."

- This man is angry because the girl accidentally knocked over some boxes at his grocery store. He says, "You're so clumsy it's amazing that you could even cross the street to get here!"

- This boy is playing with his friend outside the woman's window and making a lot of noise. She says, "You noisy brat—you don't have any consideration for other people!"

- This man says to the girl, "Boy, are you doing a crummy job trying to play that game! Why don't you just give up!"

- This boy chained his bike to this woman's fence. The woman says, "Who said you could do that? You're just a troublemaker, aren't you!"

- This man is angry and is telling the girl that she's "a spoiled brat" because she didn't share something.

You may wish to extend this learning activity by teaching Lesson #14, "What to Do When an Adult Is Angry at You," in the ASSIST manual *Helping Kids Handle Anger*.

SUPPLEMENTARY ACTIVITY #2 TRANSPARENCY

What to Say If an Adult Gives You a Put-Down

What you could say:

1. I'm sorry.

2. I'm trying to do better.

3. I feel bad when you say things like that.

What you could think:

1. I'm not bad, I'm young.

2. My behavior isn't always good, but **I'm** good.

3. Little by little, I **am** improving.

SUPPLEMENTARY ACTIVITY #3

Don't Give Yourself Put-Downs!

Your teacher will read you the sentences below.

Draw a 😊 by the things you can say to make yourself feel better.

Draw a 🙁 by the self-put-downs.

1. I'm a good kid. ◯

2. Other kids like me. ◯

3. I'm such a dummy in math! ◯

4. I'm really good at some things. ◯

5. Nobody wants to play with me. ◯

6. I hate my hair! ◯

7. I have other friends who like me. ◯

8. I don't have to have everyone for a friend! ◯

9. I may not be perfect, but I'm good enough! ◯

10. I'm the worst player in the class! ◯

Write two 😊 *of your own:*

11. _____ 😊

12. _____ 😊

SUPPLEMENTARY ACTIVITY #4

Cancel Out That Put-Down!

In the first box below write a put-down that someone once gave you which hurt your feelings. Then, in the second box, write what you could say to yourself that will, even now, keep that put-down from hurting.

The Put-Down

What You Could Say to Yourself

Remember,
when someone gives you a put-down,
you're O.K.!

SUPPLEMENTARY ACTIVITY #5

Does What I Say to Myself Make Me Happy or Sad?

Objective   Students will listen to examples of self-statements and determine whether they are examples of self-encouragement or of self-put-downs.

Materials   Paper plates, one or two for each student

Crayons or markers

Twigs, tongue depressors, or paint-stirring sticks—one or two for each student (optional)

Construction paper (optional)

Yarn (optional)

Stapler or glue (optional)

Procedure   Read the self-statements below, or ones that you make up, to the class. After each statement, have students hold up either a happy face or an unhappy face (made out of a paper plate) to indicate whether the statement is one that would make them feel better or feel worse when they get a put-down.

SELF-STATEMENTS

- I wish I were as good a player as he is.

- I may not be good at math, but I'm a good artist.

- My clothes are so dumb looking—I look like a dork.

- I may not have the greatest clothes, but I'm a neat person.

- She may not like me, but I'll live!

- There are other people in this class who like me.

- I must be the worst speller in the whole class.

- He's right—my hair looks like a bird's nest.

- Nobody likes me because I'm so skinny.

- I don't have to be perfect to be a neat kid.

VARIATIONS

There are a number of options you can consider using in this activity:

- You may wish to allow students to decorate their paper plate faces in a way that represents themselves—their hair, facial features, etc.

- You may have students cut eyeholes in the plates so they can hold them up as masks.

- You can attach sticks to the plates with a stapler or glue for students' use as handles for holding the masks in front of their faces.

- If you want to cut costs, have students draw the happy face on one side of a plate and the sad face on the other.

SUPPLEMENTARY ACTIVITY #6

Say Kind Things to Yourself
When You Get a Put-Down

Don't tell yourself that a put-down is true just because somebody says it
to you. Instead, when you get a put-down, say something
nice to yourself.

Help the kids below by crossing out the unkind things they are thinking about
themselves after receiving a put-down. Replace each unkind self-statement with
something kind they could say to themselves instead.

SUPPLEMENTARY ACTIVITY #7

Use Kind Words to Help Yourself or a Friend

What could you say to help yourself or a friend feel better if you got these put-downs?

1. You missed **that** problem? It was the easiest one!

   _____

2. My little brother can hit the ball better than you can!

   _____

3. Go play somewhere else. We don't want you on our team.

   _____

4. Why don't you get some new clothes? Nobody wears **that** anymore!

   _____

What could you say to help a friend who got these put-downs?

5. Nobody wants to play with **you**, Monkey-Face!

   _____

6. Ha! You got the lowest grade in the class on the science test! Dummy!

   _____

7. Hey, Dog-Breath! Did someone steal your toothbrush?

   _____

How to Stop Yourself From Giving Put-Downs

Objective   Students will learn techniques to help them change their put-down behaviors.

Materials   Blank transparencies and marker

Transparency #1/Poster #1 – "Things You Can Do Instead—1"

Transparency #2/Poster #2 – "Things You Can Do Instead—2"

Transparency #3/Poster #3 – "Things You Can Do Instead—3"

Transparency #4 – "The Things You Can Do Instead of Giving a Put-Down"

To the Teacher

This lesson teaches students several techniques they can use to break themselves from the habit of giving put-downs. These include using inner speech, getting their minds on something else, and choosing to have a positive interaction instead of giving a put-down.

Students who have developed the habit of relating to their peers by giving put-downs will need a great deal of encouragement and practice to change their behavior. The Supplementary Activity at the end of the lesson, which has scenarios appropriate for 1st, 2nd, and 3rd grade students, can provide additional practice with the lesson concepts.

Lesson Presentation

REVIEW OF PREVIOUS LESSONS

So far you have learned some powerful techniques for handling put-downs. You've learned that you can ignore them, or you can use your imagination to keep them from hurting you. You've also learned some clever things to say to surprise put-downers so they can't think of what to say next.

Put-downs hurt friendships, and they make others feel badly. It's easy to see why kids don't want to be friends with someone who puts them down or insults them. Still, a lot of kids give put-downs. If

you're one of those kids, today you're going to learn some ways to stop yourself from giving put-downs.

TRICKS THAT CAN HELP A PUT-DOWNER STOP GIVING PUT-DOWNS

Transp. #1

Maybe you've just gotten into the habit of giving put-downs, but you don't really want to be a put-downer. If you don't <u>want</u> to be a put-downer, there are some things you can do to help yourself stop giving put-downs. *Put Transparency #1, "Things You Can Do Instead—1," on the overhead, covering the words "Different is O.K." and "Put-downers are hard to like."* For example, you can <u>talk to yourself</u> about how it would feel if someone were to give you a put-down.

Uncover "Different is O.K." Or you can remind yourself that "different" is O.K. and that there's not just one right way to be. Just because someone doesn't look the way you think he or she should doesn't mean that person doesn't look good.

Everybody has a right to be the way they are. No one deserves a put-down because he or she is different from you.

Uncover "Put-downers are hard to like." You can also remind yourself that put-downers are hard to like and that you don't want everyone to think of you as a mean bully who picks on people.

Transp. #2

By talking to yourself in these ways, you'll probably be able to convince yourself to not give a put-down. Here's another thing you can do to stop yourself from giving a put-down—you can get your mind on something else. *Put Transparency #2, "Things You Can Do Instead—2," on the overhead.* This put-downer <u>really</u> wants to ask this kid if he just stepped off a spaceship from Mars, but he doesn't want to be a put-downer. To stop himself from giving a put-down he quickly <u>gets his mind on something else</u>. He's decided to go talk to a friend. He could have decided to finish his spelling or to go get a drink of water. Can you think of some other things he could do instead of giving a put-down? How could he get his mind on something else? *Allow students to brainstorm ways the put-downer could take his mind off giving a put-down.*

Transp. #3 | **Good! Those are some great ways of stopping yourself from giving a put-down! Here's one more trick you can use when you feel like giving a put-down—you can come up with something nice to say instead.** *Put Transparency #3, "Things You Can Do Instead—3," on the overhead.* **This girl is thinking of a put-down.** *Read "You dork! You can't even color inside the lines" from the transparency.* **But the girl knows she wants to stop giving put-downs, so she decides to use the "Look for Something Nice to Say" trick. With this trick, you don't just make something up. You think of something you notice that you like and you say something about that instead of the put-down. The trick works like magic! Instead of feeling like a mean put-downer, you feel like you're a nice kid!**

The girl shown here decides to comment on the colors the other kid has chosen. *Read "Hey, I like the colors you picked" from the transparency.* **How do you think both girls feel?**

When you <u>feel</u> like giving a put-down, you have a <u>choice</u>.

1. **Say nothing.**

2. **Say something mean by giving your put-down.**

3. **Say something nice (friendly).**

For example, if someone next to you has just colored a picture and has colored outside the lines, you could:

1. **Say nothing.**

2. **Say, "You can't even stay inside the lines."**

3. **Say, "I like the colors you picked for the person's clothes."**

If a person on your baseball team misses a fly ball, you could:

1. **Say nothing.**

2. **Say, "You klutz! My grandmother catches better than you."**

3. **Say, "Hey! You tried as hard as you could."**

Let me give you some examples of situations where you might be tempted to give a put-down. For each example, think about something nice you could say instead. Raise your hand when you come up with something. *(Some prompts are given in parentheses. You may want to give students those examples to assist them in thinking of possible replies.)*

- **Your friend has a new haircut that you think looks weird.** *("It's O.K. to try something new. Your hair will always grow and then you can change the style.")*

- **Your friend is using his dad's backpack and it looks funny because it is way too big for him.** *("It looks like you're strong enough to carry two of my backpacks.")*

- **Your friend misspells a word that you think is really easy to spell.** *("Cheer up! You're good at math/science/etc.")*

- **Your friend can't remember her address.** *("Remembering addresses is hard.")*

- **A friend is nervous and makes a lot of mistakes in a report he reads in front of the class.** *("That map you drew was great!")*

- **In P.E. a friend trips and falls during a running relay.** *("You sure tried your best!")*

(Alternatively, you could use examples from your own classroom encounters.)

PRACTICING THINGS TO DO INSTEAD OF GIVING PUT-DOWNS

Transp. #4

Now, let me tell you some about some kids who have a put-down right on the tip of their tongue. Imagine that the kids are in your class. You can help them not be mean by telling them about one of the techniques we've just been talking about. For each example, tell me what you might say to your classmate. *(Show Transparency #4 to help the students decide what technique to use. If you have any puppets, you can use them to be the following characters.)*

The first kid's name is Betty. She has just noticed that the girl who sits next to her is wearing a top that she thinks looks really weird. She feels like saying, "Is that your Halloween costume?" How can she keep herself from giving a put-down? *(Allow for student response.)*

Thompson is sitting next to a kid in the lunchroom who's eating a sardine sandwich. Thompson thinks it smells rotten and that those little fish fins look disgusting. He wants to say to the kid, "Did you steal that lunch from a Martian? Go bury it before we all throw up!" He thinks that his put-down is really clever. How can he stop himself from being mean? *(Allow for student response.)*

Neil thinks that a girl in his class is bigger than she should be. He doesn't realize that any size is O.K. When she walks by him he feels like calling her "The Incredible Hulk." How can he stop himself from hurting her feelings? *(Allow for student response.)*

IT'S HARD TO BREAK THE PUT-DOWN HABIT

You've done a very good job helping these kids break the put-down habit. Even though some of them have come up with pretty funny put-downs, they've decided they don't want to be put-downers just to get a laugh. Giving put-downs is a hard habit to break, and these kids will need to practice these techniques to change it.

We'll need to practice, too. During the next week, let's try really hard to kick the put-down habit. I'll put these posters up to help us remember things we can do instead of giving put-downs. *Show them Posters #1, #2, and #3 ("Things You Can Do Instead").* If you're able to stop yourself from giving a put-down by using one of these techniques, I'd like you to come up and whisper that you've done so in my ear. I want to be the first one to congratulate you!

LESSON REVIEW

Review the lesson by asking students to tell you what they've learned. To help reinforce the lesson concepts, you may wish to hang up Poster #1 from Lesson 1, "Don't Give Put-Downs."

SUPPLEMENTARY ACTIVITY

Use the Supplementary Activity that follows this lesson to provide additional practice of the skills taught in the lesson. The activity is appropriate for 1st, 2nd, and 3rd grade students.

Things You Can Do Instead

1.
Talk to yourself.

Put-downers are hard to like.

Different is O.K.

How would I feel?

TRANSPARENCY #2/POSTER #2

Things You Can Do Instead

2.

Get your mind on something else.

Things You Can Do Instead

3.
Use the "Look For Something Nice to Say" trick.

The Things You Can Do Instead of Giving a Put-Down

1. Talk to yourself. Say:

2. Get your mind on something else.

3. Look for something nice to say.

SUPPLEMENTARY ACTIVITY

Breaking the Put-Down Habit

Objective Students will practice choosing one of the three techniques taught in the lesson to break the habit of giving put-downs and describe possible alternative behaviors.

Materials Supplementary Activity Teacher Sheets #1A and #1B, "Scenarios"
Posters #1, #2, and #3 from the lesson, "Things You Can Do Instead"
Puppets Daphne and Thompson (optional)

Procedure The same procedure can be used for 1st, 2nd, and 3rd graders. Read the following scenarios, one at a time, or make up examples of your own. Then move around the room calling on students to help the put-downer described in the scenario choose one of the behavior techniques from the lesson (talk to yourself, get your mind on something else, say something nice instead) to break the put-down habit. Ask students to give examples of the alternative behavior the person could do, such as asking how it would feel to get a put-down (talk to yourself); going to the water fountain to get a drink (get your mind on something else); or saying, "I like the colors you chose" (look for something nice to say). Move quickly from student to student, telling those who don't offer a response that you'll come back to them later. Remind students to refer to the three posters for ideas. (You may wish to use puppets to represent the put-downers.)

VARIATION

After you have read a scenario and called on a student to respond, specify which of the three techniques you want the student to use in helping the person to do something else instead of giving a put-down.

SUPPLEMENTARY ACTIVITY TEACHER SHEET #1A

Scenarios

A boy on Thompson's baseball team strikes out when the bases are loaded, making the team lose the game. When the team gets together afterward, Thompson is so mad he wants to say, "You're such a wimp! Get lost, Loser!" How can he stop himself from giving that put-down?

Daphne is coloring a picture. She goes to the water fountain to get a drink, and when she comes back to her desk she notices the boy next to her is using her green crayon. She feels like yelling, "Give that back, you stealer!" How can she stop herself from giving that put-down?

Daphne notices that a girl in her class has just gotten her hair cut short. She thinks the girl's new hairstyle makes her look ugly. During recess she wants to say, "Go play with the boys. You look like one." How can she stop herself from giving that put-down?

Thompson is almost finished with his math problems when he notices that the boy next to him is only on the second problem. He wants to say, "Boy, are you **slow**. Are you stupid or were you just born without a brain?" How can he stop himself from giving that put-down?

During show-and-tell, one of the girls in Daphne's class shares a favorite toy. It is one that Daphne played with in preschool. She feels like saying, "That's not a neat toy. That's a baby toy." How can she stop herself from giving that put-down?

Thompson and a friend are having a disagreement about the rules of a kick ball game they are playing together. Thompson's friend is being very bossy and insists that his way is the only right way to play. Thompson is so mad he wants to shout, "Play by yourself, then, Boss-face!" How can he stop himself?

In the lunchroom, a girl who wears very thick glasses accidentally bumps Daphne's tray, sending food flying everywhere. Even though the girl apologizes and offers to help clean up the mess, Daphne is furious. She feels like saying, "Nice move, Klutz. Why don't you get a cane to help you see where you're going?" How can she stop herself from being so mean?

Daphne's little sister has been a real pest all day. Finally Daphne's mother puts the little girl to bed early and Daphne is able to watch her favorite TV show in peace and quiet. When her little sister says "Good night" to her, Daphne feels like saying, "I'm glad the pest control is finally getting rid of you." How can she stop herself from putting her little sister down?

A boy in Thompson's class seems to do everything well. He is good at almost every sport and usually gets all the answers right on his schoolwork. Even though the boy is nice to him, Thompson can't stand him and wants to call him "Mr. Perfect." How can Thompson keep himself from being mean?

Another student in Thompson's class is from a foreign country. The way he talks and dresses is different from the other boys in the class. Thompson thinks the kid is weird and feels like imitating the way he looks and talks to make the rest of the kids laugh. How can he stop himself?

SUPPLEMENTARY ACTIVITY TEACHER SHEET #1B

Scenarios (continued)

Daphne and another student are working on a poster together. The other student is having trouble drawing and writing neatly. Daphne feels like saying that her little brother could do a better job of writing and drawing. How can she stop herself from giving this put-down?

A girl in Daphne's class has a new pair of athletic shoes. Daphne thinks they are out of style and feels like asking her if her mother bought them at a garage sale. How can she stop herself from saying something so mean?

A boy in Thompson's class has brought one of his favorite games to school. He is trying to get some kids to play it with him. Thompson thinks it looks boring and wants to say, "That's a baby game." How can he stop himself?

Daphne is giving a report in front of the class. She is nervous and is having trouble reading the report. She hears someone start to snicker. She feels like saying to the student, "Shut-up, Moose-Mouth. At least I'm not a laughing hyena." How can she stop herself from giving that put-down?

Helping Kids Handle Put-Downs

Intermediate Version

Introduction to Intermediate Lessons

In these lessons students learn how to handle put-downs in an assertive but nonaggressive way using the verbal techniques of agreeing with the insult, giving a "crazy compliment" in return, or making a joke of the put-down. These three types of responses disarm the antagonizer and deflect aggression. And because they are playful retorts, they also have the potential of winning respect and leaving a way open for friendship.

Included in this section for intermediate students is a pre- and posttest on handling put-downs which you may wish to use as an evaluation tool. It would also serve as a good "anticipatory set" to begin the first lesson. Following the pre- and posttest is a letter to parents and guardians regarding ways they can help their children deal with put-downs. This letter informs parents and guardians of the goals of the unit and provides information to help them teach as well as reinforce unit skills and concepts.

You may extend the lessons by reading to your class one or more of the fiction books about teasing or put-downs from the list at the end of this Introduction.

Finally, you may wish to hang in your classroom the two posters found at the end of Lesson 2.

Pretest and Posttest on Handling Put-Downs

Directions: Circle the letter preceding the correct answer.

1.   One of the reasons that people put others down is:
      a. They've had their feelings hurt a lot themselves.
      b. They don't like themselves very much.
      c. They are trying to improve others.
      d. All of the above.

2.   What's the best thing to do if kids give you a put-down?
      a. Say mean things back to get even.
      b. Cry so they'll feel sorry for you.
      c. Ignore the put-down.
      d. Believe what they said.

3.   A way of discouraging a put-downer from continuing is:
      a. To make a joke out of the put-down.
      b. To agree with the put-downer in a humorous way.
      c. To give the put-downer a "crazy compliment."
      d. All of the above.

4.   If you insult someone who gives you a put-down, that person will probably:
      a. Turn around and leave.
      b. Put you down again.
      c. Feel sorry for what he said.
      d. Report you to the principal.

5.   An example of an effective thing to say if you get a put-down is:
      a. "Nice of you to notice."
      b. "I hate your guts."
      c. "Shut up, you creep."
      d. "That goes double for you."

6.   A helpful thing you could say to yourself about a person who puts you down is:
      a. "She's just trying to impress the other kids."
      b. "I won't give him the satisfaction of making me mad."
      c. "Something else must be bugging that kid."
      d. All of the above.

Pretest and Posttest on Handling Put-Downs (continued)

7. If a kid calls you a name
   a. It must be true.
   b. You should call her a name back.
   c. It would be best to ignore the kid.
   d. You should punch him out.

8. A boy doesn't like it when his friend teases him about his braces. It would be a good idea for him to:
   a. Not be friends with this person anymore.
   b. Make a joke about it.
   c. Ask someone else to tell his friend how he feels.
   d. None of the above.

9. When somebody teases you, it often helps to:
   a. Ignore the teasing.
   b. Think the person doesn't like you.
   c. Think the person is stupid and no good.
   d. Believe the teasing.

10. You can show a put-downer that her put-down didn't bother you by saying:
    a. "Same to you!"
    b. "I'm going to tell the teacher!"
    c. "Shut up, Jerk-Face!"
    d. "Hey! Nice eyebrows!"

11. Which response is **not** an example of agreeing with a put-down?
    a. "That was supposed to be a secret."
    b. "Yep, that's me all over!"
    c. "Frankly, that's my best quality."
    d. "Hey, that's a put-down."

12. Choose the **two** joking responses that fit this put-down: "Hey, Octopus-Breath!"
    a. "I was actually hoping to do a little worse."
    b. "Stop! You're breaking my heart!"
    c. "Will there be a test on this information?"
    d. "I was hoping you'd notice."

Pretest and Posttest on Handling Put-Downs
Answer Key

1. One of the reasons that people put others down is:
   a. They've had their feelings hurt a lot themselves.
   b. They don't like themselves very much.
   c. They are trying to impress others.
   d. All of the above.

2. What's the best thing to do if kids give you a put-down?
   a. Say mean things back to get even.
   b. Cry so they'll feel sorry for you.
   c. Ignore the put-down.
   d. Believe what they said.

3. A way of discouraging a put-downer from continuing is:
   a. To make a joke out of the put-down.
   b. To agree with the put-downer in a humorous way.
   c. To give the put-downer a "crazy compliment."
   d. All of the above.

4. If you insult someone who gives you a put-down, that person will probably:
   a. Turn around and leave.
   b. Put you down again.
   c. Feel sorry for what he said.
   d. Report you to the principal.

5. An example of an effective thing to say if you get a put-down is:
   a. "Nice of you to notice."
   b. "I hate your guts."
   c. "Shut up, you creep."
   d. "That goes double for you."

6. A helpful thing you could say to yourself about a person who puts you down is:
   a. "She's just trying to impress the other kids."
   b. "I won't give him the satisfaction of making me mad."
   c. "Something else must be bugging that kid."
   d. All of the above.

Pretest and Posttest on Handling Put-Downs—
Answer Key (continued)

7. If a kid calls you a name
   a. It must be true.
   b. You should call her a name back.
   c. It would be best to ignore the kid.
   d. You should punch him out.

8. A boy doesn't like it when his friend teases him about his braces.
   It would be a good idea for him to:
   a. Not be friends with this person anymore.
   b. Make a joke about it.
   c. Ask someone else to tell his friend how he feels.
   d. None of the above.

9. When somebody teases you, it often helps to:
   a. Ignore the teasing.
   b. Think the person doesn't like you.
   c. Think the person is stupid and no good.
   d. Believe the teasing.

10. You can show a put-downer that her put-down didn't bother you by saying:
    a. "Same to you!"
    b. "I'm going to tell the teacher!"
    c. "Shut up, Jerk-Face!"
    d. "Hey! Nice eyebrows!"

11. Which response is **not** an example of agreeing with a put-down?
    a. "That was supposed to be a secret."
    b. "Yep, that's me all over!"
    c. "Frankly, that's my best quality."
    d. "Hey, that's a put-down."

12. Choose the **two** joking responses that fit this put-down: "Hey, Octopus-Breath!"
    a. "I was actually hoping to do a little worse."
    b. "Stop! You're breaking my heart!"
    c. "Will there be a test on this information?"
    d. "I was hoping you'd notice."

Parent/Guardian Letter

Dear Parent/Guardian,

I am writing to ask for your support as we begin a unit in our classroom which focuses on assertive strategies for dealing with put-downs. Even though we try to prevent put-downs, they are a fact of school life. When they occur, many children chant, "Sticks and stones may break my bones, but words will never hurt me," or "I'm rubber and you're glue; whatever you say bounces off me and sticks to you," but put-downs are still painful and can be devastating to self-esteem.

As a parent, you probably have encouraged your child to ignore put-downs. The ignoring technique can be very effective, especially when a child holds his or her head high and affects a nonchalant body posture that implies, "You haven't hurt me with your put-down." With training, practice, and self-confidence, ignoring can become an art. However, many children need a larger repertoire of strategies if they are to hold their own in a variety of social conflict situations. The following is a synopsis of the techniques for handling put-downs that your child will be learning in my classroom. You can help to maximize your child's learning by guiding him or her through real or imaginary situations in which he or she can practice using these strategies.

Children often find that, to save face, they need to say something when they receive a put-down. Therefore, we will be focusing on some assertive verbal responses to put-downs which do not incite retaliation and which also tend to invite respect and leave the door open for the possibility of friendship. These responses fall into three categories: agreeing with the put-down, giving a crazy compliment, and making a joke of the put-down. All three types allow a child to respond to a put-down without returning the insult and escalating the verbal conflict.

While the response of **agreeing with a put-down** may seem foreign, it doesn't imply that your child really agrees with the attacker or the put-down. It is merely an effective way for your child to surprise the aggressor, allowing your child to feel strong and composed. Fifth grade students have identified the following examples of agreeing statements as favorites:

- Amazing, but true!
- Hard to believe, isn't it?
- Nice of you to notice.
- That was supposed to be a secret!
- That's an interesting way to look at it.
- Wasn't that a great mistake?
- Disgusting, isn't it?
- That's life!
- Yep, that's me all over!

Another powerful way to deal with a put-down from a peer is to **give a "crazy compliment."** Crazy compliments tell the put-downer that his or her put-down had little effect and in fact may not even have been understood as a put-down! Many students enjoy using the following kinds of crazy compliments:

- Nice eyebrows!
- You have great ears!
- Nice shoulders!
- Nice elbows!
- I like your tonsils.
- You have great arms. I like your left one even better than your right!

A third way to deal with a put-down is to **make a joke of it**. This use of humor disarms the put-downer and gains your child respect. The following comebacks are favorites of some students:

- Watch it, or I'll call my lawyer!
- Next time I must remember to bow!
- Wish you wouldn't worry about me so much.
- Stop—you're breaking my heart!
- Would you put that in writing?
- That's #47 on my list of things to fix.
- Cool your jets, man!
- Wait! Come back! There's a part of my face you haven't stepped on yet!

Finally, you can give your child a gift for life by encouraging your child to **talk to himself or herself as a good friend would** when he or she is hurting from a put-down. Making positive and truthful self-statements can keep your child from dwelling on hurtful comments. By reminding themselves of their strengths and good qualities children can sustain their self-esteem at an especially vulnerable moment. Many students have found the following self-statements helpful in keeping put-downs from hurting:

- I know I'm a neat kid.
- Other people like me.
- They don't know what I'm really like.
- No matter what they say, I'm O.K.
- I'm not going to let this bother me.
- I know I'm a good person.
- He only sees me on the outside.

By encouraging your child to agree with put-downs, give crazy compliments in response to put-downs, or make a joke of put-downs, you will enable him or her to be assertive (rather than aggressive or passive) with peers. By reminding your child to use the self-care technique of self-encouragement, you will enable him or her to keep put-downs from eroding self-esteem.

Sincerely,

Intermediate Fiction Books on Teasing and Put-Downs

Burch, R.J. (1968). *Queenie Peavy*. New York: Puffin Books.

Cunningham, J. (1970). *Burnish me bright*. New York: Pantheon.

Estes, E. (1974). *The hundred dresses*. Orlando: Harcourt Brace Jovanovich.

Giff, P.R. (1984). *The girl who knew it all*. New York: Dell.

La Farge, P. (1967). *The gumdrop necklace*. New York: Knopf.

Paterson, K. (1979). *Bridge to Terabithia*. New York: Avon.

Sachs, M. (1971). *The bears' house*. New York: E.P. Dutton.

Speare, E.G. (1972). *The witch of Blackbird Pond*. New York: Yearling.

Using Agreeing, Crazy Compliments, and Joking to Respond to Put-Downs

Objective   Students will learn to handle put-downs in a manner that does not erode their self-esteem by using the techniques of agreeing, giving crazy compliments, and joking as ways to respond to put-downs.

Materials   Transparency #1 – "Something That Can Hurt Your Self-Esteem"

Transparency #2 – "You Can IGNORE a Put-Down"

Transparency #3 – "Trick #1—AGREE With the Put-Downer"

Transparency #4/Handout #1 – "What to Say When You Get a Put-Down: AGREE With the Put-Downer"

Transparency #5 – "Trick #2—Give a CRAZY COMPLIMENT"

Transparency #6/Handout #2 – "What to Say When You Get a Put-Down: Give a CRAZY COMPLIMENT"

Transparency #7 – "Trick #3—Make a JOKE of It"

Transparency #8/Handout #3 – "What to Say When You Get a Put-Down: Make a JOKE of It"

Teacher Sheets #1A and #1B – "Some Insults to Use for Guided Practice in Assertive Responses to Put-Downs"

Handouts #4A and #4B – "Pick the Best Responses to These Put-Downs"

Handout #5 – "Ways to Answer a Put-Down"

"Put-Downer Mask" (from Supplementary Activity #3) or puppet

Transparency marker

To the Teacher

Both this lesson and Lesson 2 deal with the topic of put-downs in the classroom. Put-downs are one of the major ways children's self-esteem can be diminished. In this lesson students will learn how to handle put-downs in an assertive but nonaggressive way using the verbal techniques of agreeing with the insult, giving a crazy compliment in return, and making a joke of the put-down. These three types of responses not only can disarm the antagonizer and deflect aggression, but they are also playful retorts that have the potential of winning respect and leaving a way open for friendship. Perhaps most important, these types of responses help students maintain their self-esteem.

It may be difficult for some students to let go of their old patterns of responding to a put-down with another put-down. Should they respond with a put-down during practice sessions, it will be important to label the response as a put-down and to point out that this kind of response usually brings only more put-downs in return. It also makes their behavior just as bad as that of the put-downer.

It is helpful to give the students a copy of Handout #1 ("What to Say When You Get a Put-Down—AGREE With the Put-Downer"), Handout #2 ("What to Say When You Get a Put-Down—Give a CRAZY COMPLIMENT"), and Handout #3 ("What to Say When You Get a Put-Down—Make a JOKE of It") so they can refer to the sample responses during practice sessions.

When practicing put-downs with students, use a puppet to deliver the put-downs so that students will realize that you are only role-playing. You may wish to use the put-down list entitled "Some Insults to Use for Guided Practice in Assertive Responses to Put-Downs" as a resource when you help students practice responding to put-downs.

The skills taught in this lesson, especially the joking technique, will require a great deal of practice and reinforcement before becoming second nature to most students.

Having students complete the Supplementary Activities that follow this lesson will provide the practice necessary for the students to internalize the techniques that have been taught so that they may transfer them to real-life situations.

Lesson Presentation

IGNORING A PUT-DOWNER

Transp. #1

Today we're going to talk about how to deal with something that's <u>mean</u> and can hurt your self-esteem. Let's look at a few examples and see if you can guess what I'm talking about. *Show Transparency #1, "Something That Can Hurt Your Self-Esteem," uncovering the frames one at a time and reading them aloud. Ask students to hold up their hands as soon as they think they know what the hurtful behavior is. Call on a student volunteer to state the behavior.*

You're right! These kids are giving other kids <u>put-downs</u>. A put-down is something someone says to someone else that makes the person feel bad. A put-down can be calling someone a name she doesn't like *(write "name-calling" on frames #1 and #3)* **or making someone feel bad about something he can't do very well** *(write "making fun" on frames #2 and #4).*

Why do you think some people say cruel things to others? *Allow for student response. If students don't mention it, point out that put-downers often* *have an inability to respect differences, a need to impress other kids, or a need to seem clever or powerful.*

Most kids don't like to be friends with someone who puts them down or insults them. How many of you feel that way? *Ask for a show of hands.* **Sometimes it takes us by surprise when someone gives us a put-down. It makes us mad, and we don't know what to say or do. Do any of you ever feel that way when someone gives you a put-down?** *Ask for a show of hands.*

The easiest thing to do when someone gives you a put-down is to give one back. But that just makes you a put-downer, too, and no one really likes being mean. Today we're going to talk about some ways you can deal with a put-downer without becoming a put-downer yourself.

IGNORING A PUT-DOWN

Transp. #2

One of the best things to do when someone gives you a put-down is to merely ignore it. When you ignore a put-down, you don't bother to say anything. You just go on with what you're doing. *Show Transparency #2, "You Can IGNORE a Put-Down."* **Or, if you want to, you can give the put-downer a "give me a break" eye-roll like the girl in this picture. She's thinking about how <u>immature</u> the put-downer is. Let's all practice an eye-roll right now.** *Model this for the class.*

THE NEED TO RESPOND TO A PUT-DOWN

Ignoring a put-downer, perhaps giving him or her the "give me a break" eye-roll, is a very powerful way to respond, but every once in a while you may feel the need to say something back to a kid who is putting you down. So . . . what can you say to a put-downer that isn't just another put-down? I have some tricks that you might like to try the next time someone insults you.

AGREEING WITH THE PUT-DOWNER

Transp. #3

The first trick may come as a surprise—you <u>agree</u> with the put-downer. It may sound weird, but you'll be surprised at how well it

works. Let me show you what I mean. *Put Transparency #3, "Trick #1—AGREE With the Put-Downer," on the overhead, uncovering each frame one at a time. Discuss the response to each put-down, noting that the response is not a put-down but rather a statement of* agreement *with the put-down. Ask students:* **How do you think the put-downers felt when the kids they insulted didn't get mad?** *Point out that agreeing responses leave put-downers with nothing to say.*

Agreeing with put-downers really takes them by surprise, and they often can't think of what to say next. When you agree with a put-downer, it doesn't mean you think the put-downer is <u>right</u>**; it just means that you refuse to let the put-downer get to you—you refuse to get mad and give a put-down back. Just imagine how a put-downer would feel if you agree with her in a cool, confident way! It would really get on her nerves!**

A LIST OF AGREEING RESPONSES

Transp. #4
Handout #1

I have a list of agreeing responses you can use when a put-downer tries to make you mad. Let's look at the list and see which ones are your favorites. *Show Transparency #4, "What to Say When You Get a Put-Down: AGREE With the Put-Downer," uncovering and reading one response at a time. Add appropriate student suggestions in the spaces provided. After reviewing all of the responses on the list, you may wish to take a class poll, allowing students to vote for their two favorite responses. Tally the votes beside the number preceding each response. Then give the students a copy of Handout #1, "What to Say When You Get a Put-Down: AGREE With the Put-Downer," so that they can refer to the responses during practice sessions.*

Let's practice the agreeing technique. You'll need a piece of notebook paper. Fold it in half so you have two large rectangles on the front and two on the back, like this. *Demonstrate.* **You'll also need something to write with.** *Allow students time to prepare their materials for this exercise.*

This is how we'll practice the trick of agreeing with a put-down. This puppet will give the whole class a put-down. Then each of you should choose one of the agreeing comments from the list that you think would be a good response and write it in one of the blocks on your

paper. Make sure that the response you choose <u>fits</u> the put-down. For instance, if I said, "You look like you escaped from the zoo," it wouldn't make sense to agree by saying, "Yeah, wasn't that a great mistake?" So think carefully before you choose. I'll give you plenty of time to write before we all show our responses.

Use the following four put-downs or make up four of your own. Read them one at a time, and give students time to choose an agreeing response for each one. After students have written their response to a put-down on their papers, give them the opportunity to hold their papers at chest level. Ask a few students to share their responses, discussing with them whether their responses "fit" the put-down.

- **Your hair looks like last year's birds' nests!**

- **We would have won the game if it hadn't been for you!**

- **Hey, Monkey-Ears!**

- **Your brain is so small, it can't be seen by the human eye!**

After the practice session, say or paraphrase: **I think you're getting the idea. I'd like you to try the agreeing technique the next time you get a put-down and tell me what happens.**

GIVING A "CRAZY COMPLIMENT"

Transp. #5

I have another trick I think you'll like. This one can be great fun, and you can really use your imagination. *Put Transparency #5, "Trick #2—Give a CRAZY COMPLIMENT," on the overhead, covering all but the first frame.* **This technique really bugs put-downers because it shows them you aren't bothered by their put-downs. You give them a "crazy compliment"! They will be so surprised by your crazy compliment, they may think you didn't even notice the put-down!** *Read and explain the first frame, asking questions like the following:* **How do you think the put-downer felt when the boy told her she had great eyebrows? Do you think that was the kind of response she expected? Does the boy she put down look upset, or does he look calm and confident?** *Read and discuss the remaining three frames in the same way.*

Giving put-downers a crazy compliment really takes them by surprise, doesn't it? When you give them a crazy compliment, they know their put-down didn't get to you.

A LIST OF CRAZY COMPLIMENTS

Transp. #6
Handout #2

Put Transparency #6, "What to Say When You Get a Put-Down: Give a Crazy Compliment," on the overhead, covering up all but the first response. **Here's a list of crazy compliments you can use to surprise put-downers. Let's read the crazy compliments and see which ones you like the best.** *Uncover the crazy compliments one at a time and read them to the students, adding student suggestions at the bottom of the transparency. Have students vote for their two favorites. Tally the votes next to each crazy compliment.*

Let's practice giving some crazy compliments. *Give students copies of Handout #2, "What to Say When You Get a Put-Down: Give a Crazy Compliment," so they can refer to the responses.* **I'll give you some put-downs, and I want you to raise your hand if you want to give me a crazy compliment in response. You may use one of the crazy compliments from the list or make up your own.** *Read the following four put-downs or four put-downs you've made up, one at a time, and have students raise their hands to give their crazy compliments:*

- **You look like an octopus when you jump rope!**

- **Hey, Rabbit-Teeth! Want a carrot?**

- **Nice poster! I didn't know you could draw with your toes!**

- **Your feet are so big I'll bet you don't even need swim fins when you go to the pool!**

After the practice session, say or paraphrase: **Great! Isn't that a fun technique? And it's a pretty easy one to use, too. Try it the next time you get a put-down and tell me what happens.**

MAKING A JOKE OF THE PUT-DOWN

Transp. #7

I have one more trick I think you'll want to try. You'll have a lot of fun with this one. *Put Transparency #7, "Trick #3—Make a JOKE of It," on the overhead, covering all but the first frame.* **This technique is probably**

the most annoying of all to the put-downer—you make a <u>joke</u> of the put-down! *Read and discuss the first frame, asking questions like the following:* **How do you think the put-downer felt when his put-down was made into a joke? Do you think he got what he wanted? Does the girl look upset, or does she look calm and confident?** *Read and discuss the remaining three frames in the same way.*

If these put-downers wanted to have fun by making other kids mad, their plan didn't work. Their put-downs were <u>useless</u> when the kids made jokes of them. Joking about what a put-downer says makes you look tough and clever at the same time. It shows that the put-downer can't "get to you."

A LIST OF JOKING COMEBACKS

Transp. #8
Handout #3

Put Transparency #8, "What to Say When You Get a Put-Down: Make a JOKE of It," on the overhead, covering everything but the first response. **Here's a list of funny comebacks you can use when someone gives you a put-down. Let's read the comebacks and see which ones you like the best.** *Uncover the joking responses one at a time and read them to the students, allowing them to vote for their two favorites. Tally the votes next to each response.*

Although a lot of kids think this technique of foiling a put-downer is the most fun, it's also the hardest because you have to be able to think of a joke in a flash. Also, just as with the agreeing technique, your comeback has to fit the put-down. For instance, if someone said, "Only preschoolers wear shoes like yours!" you wouldn't want to say, "And now for my next amazing trick . . . ." That wouldn't make sense. Which comeback from the list would fit a put-down like "Only pre-schoolers wear shoes like yours"? *Allow for student response.*

Let's practice again like we did with the agreeing trick, only this time when I give a put-down, everyone should come up with a comeback that would make a joke of the put-down. *Give students copies of Handout #3, "What to Say When You Get a Put-Down: Make a JOKE of It," so they can refer to the responses. Then direct students to fold another sheet of paper in half to make two boxes on the front and two on the back. Read the following four put-downs or four that you've made up, one at a time, and have* *students write their comebacks in the boxes. After each example, allow students to show their work and call on a few to read their comebacks in a clear, firm voice.*

- **Who helped you with your homework, your little brother?**

- **You're so dumb you probably flunked kindergarten.**

- **Where did you get that jacket? Out of a garbage can?**

- **You're such a lousy jumper, no one wants to jump rope with you.**

PRACTICING WITH A PUPPET OR "PUT-DOWNER MASK"

I think you're starting to catch on to these tricks for handling put-downs. Let's practice a little more. You'll probably want to refer to your copies of the agreeing comments, the crazy compliments, and the joking comments while we practice.

This is how we're going to practice. I'm going to pretend I'm a put-downer, and I'll walk around the room giving put-downs. If I give you one, you should respond with an agreeing response, a crazy compliment, or a joking response. Remember to choose responses that fit the put-downs.

Put-Downer Mask or Puppet Teacher Sheets #1A and #1B

Use a puppet for delivering the put-downs or make a "Put-Downer Mask" using the instructions and ideas found in Supplementary Activity #3 ("Role-Playing With Masks"). Move quickly around the room using the "Put-Downer Mask" or puppet to give put-downs to individual students.

You may find that some students have settled on a couple of all-purpose comments, such as "You made my day" or "You're breaking my heart!" Encourage them to use <u>all three</u> strategies. If a student seems stymied, call on help from the class. For this exercise, use the following put-downs, the put-downs in Teacher Sheets #1A and #1B, ("Some Insults to Use for Guided Practice in Assertive Responses to Put-Downs"), or make up some of your own.

- **I wish you were on TV so I could change the channel.**

- **Your feet are so big you should wear cereal boxes for shoes.**

- **Your writing looks like a five-year-old's!**

- Your teeth are a really nice shade of green!

- Your outfit looks like your little brother picked it out!

- How long did you have to practice to be so clumsy?

- That's a nice shirt! Which trash can did you find it in?

- My little sister can read faster than you can!

- We don't want you on our team; you couldn't catch a ball if it was covered with glue!

- If I had a face like yours, I'd put a paper bag over it out of kindness to others.

- I can't believe you made such a low grade! That was such an <u>easy</u> test!

- Your notebook looks like it survived a tropical storm.

- We don't want you on our team; you're the worst player in the class.

- Are you always so klutzy, or is this a special occasion?

- Do you take ugly lessons, or does it just come naturally?

- My <u>fish</u> is smarter than you are!

- Look, everybody! A baboon has escaped from the zoo! Oh, sorry—I didn't recognize you for a minute!

After the practice session, say or paraphrase: It takes a lot of practice to be ready with a quick answer that makes you look tough and clever but isn't a put-down. We'll be practicing these tricks some more during this coming week. Then when someone gives any of you a put-down, you'll be ready!

I'd like everyone to take a minute to circle your favorite comeback on each of the lists from this lesson. After you do that, put the lists in a place in your notebook where you can glance at them often. Saying the comebacks to yourself now and then will help you remember them when you need to.

LESSON REVIEW

Have students complete Handouts #4A and #4B, "Pick the Best Responses to These Put-Downs," and Handout #5, "Ways to Answer a Put-Down," so that you can assess their understanding of the lesson. You may elect to have students complete these in class or as homework assignments.

Review the lesson by having students respond verbally to one or more of the following sentence stems:

- *I learned . . . .*

- *I was surprised . . . .*

- *I liked . . . .*

- *I wish . . . .*

SUPPLEMENTARY ACTIVITIES

Use the following Supplementary Activities to provide additional practice of the skills taught in this lesson:

- *"Responses to Put-Downs"*
  (Supplementary Activity #1)

- *"Using Skits to Identify Agreeing and Joking Techniques"*
  (Supplementary Activity #2)

- *"Role-Playing With Masks"*
  (Supplementary Activity #3)

- *"Role-Play Ideas for Practicing Dealing With Put-Downs"*
  (Supplementary Activity #4)

TRANSPARENCY #1

Something That Can Hurt Your Self-Esteem

TRANSPARENCY #2

You Can IGNORE a Put-Down

TRANSPARENCY #3

Trick #1—
AGREE With the Put-Downer

TRANSPARENCY #4/HANDOUT #1

What to Say When You Get a Put-Down:
AGREE With the Put-Downer

_____ 1. You get an "A" for awareness.

_____ 2. Amazing, but true!

_____ 3. Yeah, you're right.

_____ 4. Hard to believe, isn't it?

_____ 5. Nice of you to notice.

_____ 6. Disgusting, isn't it?

_____ 7. Thanks for the compliment!

_____ 8. That's an interesting way to look at it.

_____ 9. Yeah, wasn't that a great mistake?

_____ 10. That was supposed to be a secret.

_____ 11. It's about time you noticed.

_____ 12. Why didn't I think of that?

_____ 13. Yep, that's me all over.

_____ 14. Sometimes that's true.

_____ 15. Cool, huh?

_____ 16. You made my day!

Your ideas:

_____

_____

_____

TRANSPARENCY #5

Trick #2—
Give a CRAZY COMPLIMENT

TRANSPARENCY #6/HANDOUT #2

What to Say
When You Get a Put-Down:
Give a Crazy Compliment

_____ 1. Nice eyebrows!

_____ 2. Nice nostrils!

_____ 3. Nice ears!

_____ 4. Nice shoelaces!

_____ 5. Nice elbows!

_____ 6. Nice eyelids!

_____ 7. Nice tonsils!

_____ 8. Nice arms—your left one's even better than your right!

_____ 9. *Your ideas:*

_____

_____

TRANSPARENCY #7

Trick #3—
Make a JOKE of It

TRANSPARENCY #8/HANDOUT #3

What to Say When You Get a Put-Down:
Make a JOKE of It

_____ 1. Would you put that in writing?

_____ 2. Next time I must remember to bow!

_____ 3. Wait! Come back! There's a part of my face you haven't stepped on yet!

_____ 4. Watch it, or I'll call my lawyer.

_____ 5. And now for my next amazing trick . . . .

_____ 6. Wish you wouldn't worry about me so much.

_____ 7. Will there be a test on this information?

_____ 8. That's #47 on my list of things to fix.

_____ 9. Stop—you're breaking my heart!

_____ 10. Has this been bothering you for long?

_____ 11. Thanks for the confidence booster.

_____ 12. Thanks! I've worked hard—people are finally noticing.

TEACHER SHEET #1A

Some Insults to Use for Guided Practice in Assertive Responses to Put-Downs

The following are sample put-downs. To avoid the danger of students taking them personally, use a puppet or Put-Downer Mask to deliver them. Be sure to explain that it would be really mean and very unfair for anyone to use these put-downs to hurt others.

Face, Hair, Etc.

- If I had a face like yours, I'd walk backwards.
- You're so ugly you should wear **two** bags over your head in case one rips.
- You're so ugly you have to sneak up on a mirror.
- Hey, Dog-Face!
- Hey, Cucumber-Nose!
- I like your funny hat—oh, sorry, that's your hair, isn't it!
- The best way you could improve your face is to keep the lower half shut.
- What's that horrible stuff all over your face? Oh, sorry, I guess that **is** your face.
- Hey, Pencil-Neck!
- You look just like a TV star—Alf!
- Gee, you look great! Did you have plastic surgery?
- The last time I saw a nose like yours, it was on a snowman.
- Is that your nose or are you eating a pickle?
- Hey, Orangutan—did you escape from the zoo?
- I like what you're wearing, but aren't you a little early (late) for Halloween?
- Hey Clam-Breath, get a mouthwash.

Intelligence and Coordination

- Would you like one of the kindergartners to help you with that?
- Do we laugh now or when you talk?
- Where did you get your brains? At the bird store?
- Hey, Stupid! Yeah, you!
- Are you always so stupid or is today a special occasion?
- Hey, Clumsy! Nice move!
- You're so clumsy the clowns come to you for lessons.
- Hey, Motor-Mouth!
- You're so stupid, I hear you even flunked recess.
- You should wear a sign on your head that says "Help Wanted."

Food, Lunch, Etc.

- They say you are what you eat—and that sure looks like you, alright!
- Is that your lunch, or are you taking out the garbage?
- Uh-oh—looks like your mommy forgot to pack your bottle!
- You eat like a pig with hiccups.

TEACHER SHEET #1B

Some Insults to Use for Guided Practice in Assertive Responses to Put-Downs (continued)

Sports

- Sure you can play. Lie down over there—you can be the bench.
- Is the other team paying you to be so crummy?
- My dog can catch better than you can.
- Even a skunk would think you stink.

General

- Why don't you drink some spot remover and disappear!
- I wish you were on TV so I could turn you off.
- People like you don't grow on trees—they swing from them.
- You should go to Hollywood. The walk will do you good.
- You're as gross as the stuff that grows on my shower curtain.
- Do you take dork lessons, or does being a dork just come naturally?
- Last time I saw a face like yours, I threw it a fish!
- You're so ugly your nose hangs down to your toes.

Body

- *(Pointing at student's shoes)* Oh, look, it's ski season again!
- Are you still living in the garbage dump, or is that your normal smell?
- With that face and those feet, let me guess—Bozo the Clown, right?
- Do you take **ugly pills**, or what?

Clothing

- Those are great-looking pants. Too bad they didn't have your size.
- Oh, nice clothes. Did the Salvation Army have a sale?
- I see you found your shirt after the dog tried to bury it again, huh?
- Great outfit—isn't that the same one they wear on Sesame Street?
- Is that what all the **preschoolers** are wearing this year?
- What size are those shoes? They look like army boots.
- Your mother sure dresses you funny.

Pick the Best Responses to These Put-Downs

Draw a line through the responses that are put-downs themselves. **Circle** the responses that are powerful, quick comebacks, jokes, or responses that throw the put-downer off-balance by agreeing with him or her. **Put a star** by your favorite responses.

The Put-Downs	The Responses
Would you like a kindergartner to help you with your math?	Wish you wouldn't worry about me so much. Compared to you I'm a genius, Beetle-Brain! That's an interesting way to look at it. No thanks.
You can't be in our club; it's not for dorks.	Oh, ouch! Stop—you're breaking my heart. I wouldn't be in a club with you jerks if you paid me! Gee, you're nice.
You and your dog have one thing in common—looks!	Invite me to your funeral, Dweeb! That's an interesting way to look at it. Amazing, but true! Hard to believe, isn't it?
I can't believe you could miss the easiest question on the test!	Yeah, wasn't that a great mistake! You're not so smart yourself, Motor-Mouth. Would you put that in writing? You've got a point there.
Nice move, Klutz. You can't even walk to the front of the room without tripping.	And now for my next amazing trick . . . . Yep, that's me all over. You shouldn't talk about yourself, Geek! That's life.

HANDOUT #4B

Pick the Best Responses to These Put-Downs (continued)

The Put-Downs	The Responses
Nice outfit. You could start a new style for preschoolers.	I've been working on it—people are finally noticing. Drop dead, Dog-Breath! I was hoping you'd notice. I know. Isn't it cool?
Do you take ugly pills or what?	Look in the mirror—you'll get sick. Thanks for the compliment. That was supposed to be a secret. Fun talking to you.
Your ears stick out so far you look like Dumbo.	All the better to hear you with. Has this been troubling you for long? You're gonna get it, Retard! Oh no, really?
You're such a wimp! You caused us to lose the game!	Get lost, Pizza-Face! Next time I must remember to bow. Cool your jets, man. Wasn't that a great mistake?

HANDOUT #5

Ways to Answer a Put-Down

Write responses to the following put-downs in the spaces provided.

1. Hey, Fudge-Brain! _____

   _____

2. Yo, Banana-Nose! _____

   _____

3. You're so ugly you need to wear two bags over your head in case one rips.

   _____

4. You must be really stupid to miss such an easy question!

   _____

5. Hey, Geek! Your ears weigh more than your brain!

   _____

6. Well, if it isn't ol' Dog-Breath!

   _____

7. Is that a monster mask or your face?

   _____

8. Nice move, Klutz!

   _____

   _____

9. Get lost, loser!

   _____

   _____

SUPPLEMENTARY ACTIVITY #1

Responses to Put-Downs

Circle your four favorite responses.
Write the response you like the best in the word bubble.

Will there be a test on this information?

Well, what do you know!

Hey, that's a put-down!

Next time I must remember to bow!

Attractive, aren't I?   Have it your way!

I was actually hoping to do it a little worse.

Frankly, that's my best quality.

No kidding!

Maybe, maybe not.

Ouch!   Funny joke!

I gotta be me.   **Whatever.**

Nice of you to notice.

And here I thought we were best friends!

That's nice to know.   **Who told you?**

Stop, I'm blushing!   Wow! You really think so?

Sorry it affects you so much!

Hey, I was just starting to like you.

Wow—I didn't know you cared.   Sorry you seem to need to hurt people.

Fun talking to you.

Gee, you're nice.

Well, it's been fun talking to ya. Bye.   That's interesting.   I like your jacket.

Give me a break! Who said I was perfect?

SUPPLEMENTARY ACTIVITY #2

Using Skits to Identify Agreeing and Joking Techniques

Objective   Students will identify the strategies used by characters in skits to de-escalate the conflict of a put-down situation.

Materials   Supplementary Activity #2 Handout #1A, Script #1
Supplementary Activity #2 Handout #1B, Script #2
Supplementary Activity #2 Handout #1C, Script #3
Supplementary Activity #2 Handout #1D, Script #4

Procedure   Students will present the skits included in this activity to the rest of the class. For each skit, the student playing the part of the person who is insulted will model responding to put-down(s) in a calm, confident manner. The rest of the class will try to name the strategy (or strategies) the student used (agreeing or joking) and try to repeat the exact words used by the assertive respondent.

SUPPLEMENTARY ACTIVITY #2 HANDOUT #1A

Script #1

Title:	"'Toothpick' Joins the Group"
Scene:	Jared is the new guy at school. He's meeting a bunch of other guys before P.E. class.
Characters:	Jared Dominic Andre Wesley

Jared (*Walks over to a group of boys on the playing field*) Hi. I'm new here. Can I play with you guys?

Dominic Yeah. What's your name? I haven't seen you around before.

Jared Jared.

Dominic (*To Andre*) I thought he'd say his name was "Toothpick," he's so skinny!

Andre Yeah! Well, his name ought to be Toothpick. Let's call him Toothpick.

Dominic Good idea! Hi, Toothpick. I'm Dominic.

Wesley Nice to meet you, Toothpick. I'm Wesley.

Andre I'm Andre, Toothpick.

Jared Hi. If I get into some sports, maybe I'll put on some weight. Then you'll have to think up a new nickname! (*Laughs*)

Wesley Where are you from, Toothpick?

Jared I'm from _____. How hard is it to get on the ball team here?

Andre It's pretty hard to get on the team. I don't think you could handle it, Toothpick.

Jared (*Laughs*) Well, I'm not Superman, but I think I can handle it.

Dominic We'll see. Want to meet the other guys?

Jared (*Smiles*) Sure!

(*All four boys walk offstage.*)

Script #2

Title: "The Slowpoke Gives a Quick Comeback"

Scene: Jasmine is still working on her seatwork assignment at her desk. The other girls are finished and are standing near her.

Characters: Jasmine   Daisy   Natasha

Daisy Natasha, I'm finished with my assignment. Want to go back to the art center and work on our science poster?

Natasha Sure. Maybe we can get it finished today. Jasmine, want to help?

Jasmine I can't. I'm not finished with my assignment.

Daisy You're not finished yet? I've been finished for ages!

Natasha Me too! It was an easy assignment.

Daisy (*Looking down at Jasmine's work*) What's taking you so long, Jasmine?

Jasmine (*Not looking up*) I'm just not finished. That's all.

Natasha Jasmine, you're always the last one finished!

Jasmine (*Continuing to work*) Shhh—let me finish . . . .

Daisy What a slowpoke!

Natasha Come on, Daisy. Everyone knows Jasmine is the slowest one in the whole class.

Jasmine (*Smiling at the other girls*) It's great to be so famous!

Script #3

Title:	"Agreeable Aaron"
Scene:	Aaron's team has just lost the ball game. Everyone is disappointed. Trent blames Aaron.
Characters:	Aaron Eugene Trent

Eugene   What a lousy game. I thought we were going to win!

Aaron   Yeah! It was cruel to lose such a close game!

Trent   (*Angrily*) It's your fault, Aaron! If you hadn't dropped that fly ball, they wouldn't have scored that last run!

Aaron   Amazing, but true!

Eugene   (*Disappointed*) Now we don't get to go to the play-offs!

Trent   (*To Eugene*) Yeah, thanks to Aaron! Not only did he drop a fly ball; he got tagged out at second!

Aaron   (*Nodding*) You're right again, Trent.

Trent   (*To Aaron, with hands on hips*) You're the worst player on the team, Aaron! If it weren't for you, we would be in the play-offs next week! What a geek!

Aaron   (*Shrugging his shoulders and looking at Trent*) What can I say, Trent? You're right! You're totally right! No one has ever been as right as you are!

Trent   (*Stalks off angrily*)

Eugene   Oh, well. . . . There's always next year. . . .

SUPPLEMENTARY ACTIVITY #2 HANDOUT #1D

Script #4

Title:	"The Artist Gets the Last Laugh"
Scene:	A group of students have prepared a report for social studies. The group members are getting ready to give their report to the class. Roberta is in charge.
Characters:	Olivia Roberta Fred Wally

Roberta	O.K. I wrote about the geography of Italy. Do all of you have your part of the report ready?
Fred	Yeah. Here's mine. I found out about all the major cities of Italy and wrote a paragraph about each one.
Wally	And I wrote two pages about the history of Italy.
Roberta	Great! Olivia, you said you'd do the map.
Olivia	I did! How do you like it? (*Shows a large map*)
Fred	(*Laughs and points*) I thought Italy was supposed to look like an old-timey boot! Your map looks like a hiking boot!
Olivia	Cool, isn't it?
Wally	(*Laughs*) Who did the lettering for you, Olivia? Your little brother?
Olivia	Actually I did it with my toes!
Roberta	Yuck! And you picked the ugliest colors there are, Olivia! (*Sticks out tongue and uses finger to make gagging sign*)
Olivia	Stop, you guys! You're breaking my heart! (*Puts hand over heart*)

SUPPLEMENTARY ACTIVITY #3

Role-Playing With Masks

Objective   Working with their Learning Partners, students will make masks and use them to practice the agreeing and joking techniques for dealing with put-downs.

Materials   Supplementary Activity #3 Transparency, "Ideas for Your Put-Downer Mask"

Supplementary Activity #3 Handout, "Put-Down Cards" (one complete set per pair of Learning Partners)

Handout #1 from the lesson, "What to Say When You Get a Put-Down: AGREE With the Put-Downer"

Handout #3 from the lesson, "What to Say When You Get a Put-Down: Make a JOKE of It"

Construction paper or paper plates

Crayons or markers

Glue and scissors

Procedure   Explain to students that they will be making masks to use for practicing the agreeing and joking techniques for responding to put-downs. The masks will help them remember not to take the put-downs personally.

Provide the students with the materials for making their masks. Show Supplementary Activity #3 Transparency, "Ideas for Your Put-Downer Mask," to stimulate their imaginations. Remind students to cut eyeholes in their masks. When their masks are completed, allow students to share their work by having everyone hold their mask up at the same time.

Ask students to sit with their Learning Partners. Each student will need his or her completed mask and a copy of Handouts #1 and #3 from the lesson. Give each pair of Learning Partners a complete set of the Put-Down Cards.

Review the agreeing and joking techniques students learned for dealing with put-downs. Then model this activity for students as follows: Borrow a student's mask. Make up a put-down. Hold up the mask and say the put-down aloud. Ask a volunteer to choose a response from one of the handouts and deliver it with a calm, confident voice. The volunteer does not use his or her mask when receiving or responding to the put-down. Repeat your modeling with other examples until you feel the students understand the procedure.

When students seem ready, have Learning Partners face one another and alternate turns playing the role of "Put-Downer" and "Responder." The

"Put-Downer" will draw a Put-Down Card and read that put-down aloud while holding his or her Put-Downer Mask in front of his or her face. The "Responder" will choose either an agreeing or a joking response from the handouts and deliver it in a calm, confident voice without using his or her mask. Learning Partners will then switch roles and begin again.

VARIATION

Have Learning Partners perform their role-plays in front of the class. The "Put-Downer" partner would hold up his or her mask and read the put-down on the Put-Down Card. The other partner would respond with an appropriate agreeing or joking response. Then they could repeat the role-play with the entire class calling out in unison the chosen response to the put-down.

SUPPLEMENTARY ACTIVITY #3 TRANSPARENCY

Ideas for Your Put-Downer Mask

SUPPLEMENTARY ACTIVITY #3 HANDOUT

Put-Down Cards

What's that horrible stuff smeared all over your face? Oh, sorry! I guess that is your face!

Your nose is so big and red it would make Rudolph jealous!

You're so ugly even the space aliens didn't want you!

Your jokes are so bad even the Three Stooges wouldn't laugh.

Your brain is so weak you have to wear crutches under your *ears!*

Your breath smells like you ate dog food for breakfast!

Last time I saw a face like yours, it was in the zoo!

You're so clumsy you can't walk and chew gum at the same time!

Nice clothes! Did the junk store have a sale?

You're such a bad ballplayer, even the kindergartners don't want you on their team!

You walk like a duck!

Your ears stick out so far you look like a car with both doors open!

Your hair looks like your little brother cut it for you!

You're so dumb you can't even add with a calculator!

SUPPLEMENTARY ACTIVITY #4

Role-Play Ideas for Practicing Dealing With Put-Downs

Pick one of the following situations. With one or more partners, decide who will give the put-down(s) and who will give a **powerful** response that's not a put-down itself. Then, role-play the situation.

You are watching TV. The cable goes out. You ask your older brother to help you fix it. He says, "Do it yourself, Stupid."	You're playing soccer. You have what looks like a perfect opportunity to get a goal, but you miss. Your teammates start calling you names.
Your class is writing books. You show your book to the group. Someone says, "That's the worst book in the class."	You want to join the swim team. You ask a boy on the swim team what it's like. He says, "**You'll** never make it! You'd probably drown!"
You crash your bike. When you ask the kid next door to help you fix it, he says, "No way—fix it yourself, Klutz!"	Your friend is answering your question about your math homework. The kid behind you starts whispering that you're stupid.
You wear the new shirt you got for your birthday to school. The kid next to you says, "Your mother sure dresses you funny!"	On your way home from school some kids start calling you names: "Hey, Tubs!"; "Four-Eyes!"; "Oyster-Brain!"

How to Keep Put-Downs From Hurting Self-Esteem: Using Self-Encouragement

Objective   Students will learn to encourage themselves with positive self-statements when they have been given a put-down.

Students will learn to encourage friends who have been put down by others.

Materials   Transparency #1 – "Say Kind But True Things to Yourself"

Transparency #2/Handout #1 – "What to Say to Yourself When You Get a Put-Down"

Teacher Sheets #1A and #1B from Lesson 1 – "Some Insults to Use for Guided Practice in Assertive Responses to Put-Downs" (optional)

Transparency #3 – "Sometimes We Give Ourselves a Put-Down"

Transparency #4 – "Which Is Better to Say to Yourself?"

Transparency #5/Handout #2 – "What Can They Say?"

Transparency #6/Handout #3 – "How to Help Someone Who Has Been Put Down"

Handout #4 – "Say Something Kind to Yourself"

Poster – "Caution: No Put-Down Zone"

Transparency marker

To the Teacher

In Lesson 1, students were taught skills they can use to defend themselves verbally from put-downs. In this lesson, students will learn things to say to themselves to make sure the put-downs do not deal a blow to their self-esteem.

Students will learn that they can choose to keep put-downs from hurting their self-esteem. They will practice making themselves feel better when they get a put-down by saying or thinking self-encouraging and **true** statements about themselves. (While statements that are exaggeratedly flattering may sound self-encouraging, they won't really help a wounded ego. A child's sense of integrity won't allow him or her to believe something that isn't true.) Students will also learn that this skill of saying something kind can be a friendship tool. They can use it to help someone else feel better after that person has received a put-down.

You may wish to use Supplementary Activity #5, "An Imaginary Letter to Someone You Tease," to encourage students who give others put-downs to stop doing so.

When you facilitate practice in nonaggressive responses to put-downs use a "cool puppet" to deliver put-downs to your class so they don't experience you putting them down. A snake or shark puppet works really well with intermediate age students. So does a "Wyle E. Coyote" puppet.

Lesson Presentation

REVIEW OF THE IGNORING, AGREEING, CRAZY COMPLIMENT, AND JOKING STRATEGIES

You've been practicing some ways of dealing with put-downers without being mean. One of the techniques you've been practicing is <u>ignoring</u> the put-downer and even giving him or her the "give me a break" eye-roll. Would someone volunteer to demonstrate the "give me a break" eye-roll? *Call on a student volunteer.* **The "give me a break" eye-roll lets the put-downer know you think he or she is acting pretty immature.**

You also learned that you can discourage a put-downer by <u>agreeing</u> with him or her. If the put-downer's goal was to upset you and get you to argue or defend yourself, he or she will be pretty disappointed if you agree with the put-down! Who can give me a favorite agreeing comment? You may want to look at your handout if you can't remember one. *Call on a couple of student volunteers to make agreeing statements.*

Another powerful way to deal with a put-down from a peer is to give a crazy compliment. Crazy compliments tell put-downers that their put-down had little effect and in fact may not even have been understood as a put-down! Many students enjoy using the following crazy compliments:

- **Nice eyebrows!**

- **You have great ears!**

- **Nice shoulders!**

- **Nice elbows!**

- **I like your tonsils.**

- **You have great arms. I like your left one even better than your right!**

The last technique we talked about is one that drives most put-downers crazy. It's the hardest to carry out sometimes, but it can be the most fun! Who can remember what that technique is? *Call on a student to tell you that the technique is to make a joke of the put-down.* Yes! Making a joke of a put-down leaves the put-downer with nothing much to say. If a put-downer wants to make you mad and you just turn the put-down into a joke, you've ruined his or her fun! What are some of your favorite joking comments? You may look at your hand-out if you can't remember. *Allow for student response.*

SAYING HELPFUL THINGS TO YOURSELF

Even though all of these techniques can help protect us from put-downs, once in a while someone will say a mean put-down that hits us hard before we have a chance to defend ourselves from it. And it hurts! When that happens, we need to find a way to make ourselves feel better.

Let's talk for a minute about what you do when you get hurt when you're playing. How many of you have ever fallen when you were jumping rope or playing ball and scraped your elbow? *Allow for a show of hands.* If you fall and scrape your elbow and it's all dirty and bleeding, you need to take care of it.

When someone says something mean to you and it makes you hurt on the inside, you need to take care of that hurt, too. Just as you might put medicine or a bandage on a scraped elbow to make it feel better, you can say kind things to yourself to make yourself feel better when you've been put down.

SAYING HELPFUL THINGS THAT ARE ALSO TRUE

Transp. #1

I'm not talking about saying things to yourself like, "I'm the best kid in the world!" or "Everyone in the whole school wants to be my friend!" I'm talking about kind statements that are also true statements; those are the only ones that really make you feel better. Let me show you some examples. *Put Transparency #1, "Say Kind But True Things to Yourself," on the overhead.*

For instance, you might say to yourself, "I'm a neat kid," or you might remind yourself, "Other people like me." *Point to these statements on the transparency.* Can you think of some other kind but true things you could say to yourself when someone has hurt you with a put-down? *Lead students in brainstorming encouraging self-statements and write as many as you can in or around the bubbles on the transparency.*

Transp. #2

Here are some other helpful comments kids have used to make themselves feel better when people have given them put-downs. Let's see which ones you like the best. Show students Transparency #2, "What to Say to Yourself When You Get a Put-Down," uncovering and reading each self-statement one at a time. Add student ideas from the previous brainstorming session on the lines provided. (You may wish to have students vote on their favorites.)

Handout #1

I'm going to give you a copy of this list so you can practice saying kind things to yourself when you get a put-down. I encourage you to look at the list whenever you need to, even after we've finished this lesson. Saying something kind to yourself really can take the sting out of a put-down. *Distribute Handout #1, "What to Say to Yourself When You Get a Put-Down," to the students. Have students put a star by their favorite statements.*

PRACTICING USING KIND BUT TRUE SELF-STATEMENTS

Lesson 1, Teacher Sheets #1A and #1B

Saying kind things to yourself is hard to practice because it all happens on the inside. So, let's do this—take out a piece of notebook paper and fold it in half two times. *Demonstrate.* You'll have four boxes on the front and four on the back. I'm going to say a put-down, and I want each of you to think of a kind but true statement you could say to yourself to make yourself feel better. Then I want you to write that statement in one of the boxes on your paper. We'll practice with a number of put-downs. After we're finished practicing, I'll collect your papers so I can see the kinds of statements you're choosing for yourselves. No one else will see your papers but me. *Allow time for students to prepare their papers.*

Are you ready? If you have trouble thinking of a kind but true statement, you may look at the transparency or at the handout I just

gave you. *Read the following put-down statements, make up some of your own, or use the put-down list from Lesson 1 (Teacher Sheets #1A and #1B), giving students time to write an encouraging self-statement on their papers after each put-down:*

- You still don't know your 7-times tables? Those are easy!

- Beat it! We don't want any dorks on our team.

- Why don't you get some new shoes? Those look like they're about 40 years old!

- Hey, Clumsy! Way to drop the ball!

- You got a "D" on your book report? "D" stands for "Dumb," you know!

- You can't sit here, Dipstick; I'm saving this seat for somebody nice!

- Hey, Beanpole! Get a life!

- My three-year-old sister can run faster than you can!

SOMETIMES WE GIVE OURSELVES PUT-DOWNS

Transp. #3

When someone gives us a put-down, it can catch us so much by surprise that we may think that the put-downer is right! We can feel so bad about ourselves that we may even give ourselves <u>another</u> put-down in our minds! *Place Transparency #3, "Sometimes We Give Ourselves a Put-Down," on the overhead.* **Listen to this story and see if something like this has ever happened to you:**

Alex's baseball team was having its turn in the field. Alex was a pretty good batter, but he wasn't the greatest fielder. He especially had trouble catching grounders. The pitcher threw a low ball and the batter swung at it. Crack! A grounder—skipping across the ground toward Alex. The ball bounced off Alex's glove and rolled past him. The first baseman groaned and said loudly, "My grandma can play ball better than you can, Alex!" Alex thought to himself, "He's right—I'm such a crummy player. Everyone thinks I'm no good."

How many of you have had an experience like that? *Allow students to share their experiences.* **Did you notice that Alex got <u>two</u> put-downs? Alex's teammate put him down for missing the catch. That was the first put-down. But who gave Alex the second put-down?** *Allow for student response. Students should observe that Alex put himself down as a bad ballplayer.*

Alex made himself feel <u>worse</u> by believing the put-downer, and he gave himself another put-down in his mind! How many of you know what that's like? *Allow for a show of hands. Ask if any students would be willing to share a story about a time when they gave themselves a put-down. You might model a self-put-down of your own.*

We often believe the put-downs we get—especially if they're a <u>little bit</u> true. In the case of Alex, it was <u>true</u> that Alex was not good at catching grounders. But he was a good batter, so it wasn't true that he was a totally bad ballplayer. And it <u>certainly</u> wasn't true that the first baseman's grandmother could play ball better than Alex! By agreeing with the put-down and giving himself another one, Alex made himself feel worse. Can anyone think of something he could have said to himself instead that would have made him feel better? *Allow for student response.*

PRACTICING RECOGNIZING SELF-PUT-DOWNS

Transp. #4

Put Transparency #4, "Which Is Better to Say to Yourself?" on the overhead, covering all but the first example. **I'm going to read you some more put-downs and some things people might say to themselves in response. Think about which of the responses would make the person feel better and which would make the person feel worse.**

Read the first put-down. **Here are some of the things the girl on the right might say to herself. Some of them could make her feel better, and some of them are self-put-downs. Let's put a "+" by the ones that could make her feel better and a "–" by the ones that could make her feel worse.** *Read the items to the right of the first put-down and allow students to identify them as helpful or unhelpful self-talk. Mark the positive responses with a plus sign and the negative responses with a minus sign. Go over the rest* *of the transparency in the same way, reading the put-down to the students and asking them to distinguish between encouraging self-talk and self-put-downs.*

I'm glad to see that you can tell the difference between self-statements that would make you feel better and ones that would make you feel worse. Remembering to say something to make yourself feel better can be a very tricky thing. Sometimes you won't even <u>know</u> that you believed the put-downer; all you'll notice is that you feel hurt. The best thing to do is to get in the habit of saying something to make yourself feel better <u>any time</u> you get a put-down.

ADDITIONAL PRACTICE AND HOMEWORK

Handout #2
Transp. #5

I'm going to give you a handout with a few situations involving kids who have been given put-downs. As we go over it, I want you to help me brainstorm some things that would make these kids feel better. *Distribute copies of Handout #2, "What Can They Say?" and show Transparency #5 of the same title.*

Let's look at the first situation. As I read it, try to think of something the person could say to himself or herself to feel better. *Read the first scenario. Ask students the following kinds of questions:* **How many of you know anyone who has ever gotten a put-down a little like this one? How do you think this person feels? What could this kid say to himself or herself to feel better? What could you say to a friend who has received a put-down like this?** *Ask students to write their best idea on the lines under the situation.*

Review the rest of the scenarios in the same manner. Then ask students to think of other put-down situations involving imaginary kids, not themselves, and share them with the class. (Students will be more likely to participate if they aren't asked to share their own humiliations but are allowed to project these and their positive self-statements onto imaginary students.) Tell students that you would like them to complete #2 on the handout for homework if they are not finished.

WE CAN HELP FRIENDS WHEN THEY GET PUT DOWN

Explain to students that knowing how to say something kind but true is a skill they can use to help their friends as well as themselves. Say or paraphrase: **Sometimes a friend of yours will get a put-down. Have you ever heard someone say something mean to one of your friends? Or do you remember a time when a friend of yours was really down and told you about a put-down someone had given to him or her?** *Allow for student response.*

Transp. #6

You can help someone else feel better using the same skill you've just learned for helping yourself. As a matter of fact, it may be easier for you to help someone else than it is for you to make yourself feel better. *Put Transparency #6, "How to Help Someone Who Has Been Put Down," on the overhead. Cover the transparency with two strips of paper so that only the two girls are showing.*

Here are two girls. One of them has just gotten a put-down and the other is helping her feel better by saying kind things to her. What could a put-downer have said to hurt this girl's feelings? *Encourage students to make up a scenario.*

Remove the paper strip covering the statements on the right side of the transparency. **Here are some things the light-haired girl might be saying to make her friend feel better.** *Read the statements. Ask students if they have any other ideas and write their ideas at the bottom of the list. Have students vote on the statement they like best and write it on the transparency in the bubble above the girl's head.*

Next, show the picture of the two boys and lead the class through the same exercise of making up a scenario and voting on a kind statement to write in the bubble.

BEING PREPARED FOR PUT-DOWNS

I hope you'll be on the lookout for put-downs this week. If anyone makes a negative comment to you, try one of the techniques we've talked about. And don't forget to say something kind but true to yourself—that's one of the best ways to keep a put-down from sticking to you. When you say encouraging things to yourself, put-downs just bounce right off.

And remember, you can be a really <u>good</u> friend to someone else who has been put down by saying something to help that person feel better.

During the next few days, you can help students remember to practice using positive self-talk to neutralize the hurt of a put-down by asking them to share instances with you when they applied this skill. You may ask them to share with you individually from time to time or to share their experiences in writing. You may wish to provide a lidded box in which students can deposit short put-down reports describing instances when they successfully used any of the skills covered in these lessons.

HOMEWORK

Give students Handout #3, "How to Help Someone Who Has Been Put Down" (copy of Transparency #6 used previously). Explain that although you have already discussed this page, you would like the students to fill in the bubbles on their own, as a homework assignment, with two of their favorite helpful comments. They may choose comments from the list or make up their own. Give students Handout #4, "Say Something Kind to Yourself," as a final homework assignment.

LESSON REVIEW

Poster

You may wish to hang the poster "Caution: No Put-Down Zone" as a reminder to students that everyone in the classroom knows how to handle put-downs, so giving a put-down would be a waste of time.

If you gave the pretest on handling put-downs at the beginning of Lesson 1, you may wish to give students the posttest now to evaluate their understanding of the concepts presented in the unit.

SUPPLEMENTARY ACTIVITIES

Use the following Supplementary Activities to provide additional practice of the skills taught in this lesson:

- *"I'm an O.K. Kid!"*
  (Supplementary Activity #1)

- *"Shielding Yourself From Put-Downs"*
  (Supplementary Activity #2)

- *"Keeping Count"*
  (Supplementary Activity #3)

- *"What to Do If an Adult Puts You Down"*
  (Supplementary Activity #4)

- *"An Imaginary Letter to Someone You Tease"*
  (Supplementary Activity #5)

TRANSPARENCY #1

Say Kind But True Things to Yourself

TRANSPARENCY #2/HANDOUT #1

What to Say to Yourself When You Get a Put-Down

Possible Thoughts or Self-Talk

- He's just trying to act cool.
- She's trying to impress the other kids. She must need friends.
- He only sees me on the outside. He doesn't know what I'm really like.
- She's trying to get to me. I'll ignore her.
- I won't give him the satisfaction of getting upset.
- She's the one with the problem.
- Someone must have hurt his feelings and he's trying to take it out on me.
- She's just trying to feel better about herself.
- Other people like me.
- I'm different than he thinks.
- *Your ideas:*

_____

_____

_____

TRANSPARENCY #3

Sometimes We Give Ourselves a Put-Down

TRANSPARENCY #4

Which Is Better to Say to Yourself?

PUT-DOWN	SELF-STATEMENT

1 Hey, Elephant-Legs! My little sister can jump better than you can!

a. I always goof up—why even try?
b. Nobody's perfect.
c. This is a stupid game—I hate it.
d. I do other things well.

2 You're so ugly the doctor ran out of the room when you were born!

a. This kid is just trying to impress her friends.
b. I wish I could just go and hide.
c. What's this kid's problem?
d. Everyone thinks I'm ugly.

3 Hey, Einstein—nice job! Maybe you can get them all wrong next time!

a. She's right—I'm just stupid.
b. No one can be a whiz at everything.
c. There's nothing I can do about this—I'm always going to look like an idiot.
d. I'm not going to let this bother me. I know I'm getting a little better.

4 Oh, what a nice coat! Did you get it out of a dumpster?

a. I hate it that I always look like a dork.
b. She's just trying to get the other kids to think she's funny.
c. Everyone is always mean to me.
d. That's just her opinion.

5 You eat like you're a human garbage disposal.

a. I can get even with her after lunch by tripping her in P.E.
b. That hurts my feelings, but I can handle it.
c. I'm a slob.
d. She just wants me to get mad.

TRANSPARENCY #5/HANDOUT #2

What Can They Say?

Read the following situations. Ask yourself what each person could say to himself or herself to feel better.

1. My parents don't have a lot of money, so I'm not able to wear the latest styles of clothes. The kids at school tease me and call me names because of my clothes.
   Helpful Self-Statement: _____

   _____

2. I have a reading problem, and everyday I have to get special help. The kids in class tease me and put me down because I get special help. Sometimes I feel like telling them off, but that won't stop them.
   Helpful Self-Statement: _____

   _____

3. I just got a perm and it turned out too curly. People keep asking me if I put my finger in a light socket. It's embarrassing.
   Helpful Self-Statement: _____

   _____

4. I'm having what my mom calls a "growth spurt," and I've gotten taller than most of the kids in my class. The kids keep asking me, "How's the weather up there?" It feels bad enough being taller than everyone else without their teasing!
   Helpful Self-Statement: _____

   _____

5. You describe the situation: _____

   _____

   _____

   Helpful Self-Statement: _____

   _____

How to Help Someone Who Has Been Put Down

- Are you O.K.?

- Don't pay any attention to them.

- Come on, let's go someplace else.

- They don't know what you're really like.

- No matter what they say, you're still my friend.

- Don't worry. I'll be your friend.

- Don't feel bad. You have other friends.

- We all make mistakes. I'm still your friend.

Your ideas:

_____

_____

HANDOUT #4

Say Something Kind to Yourself

Write what you could say to help yourself feel better if you got these put-downs.

1. You missed **that** problem? It was the easiest one!
   _____
   _____

2. My little brother can hit the ball better than you can!
   _____
   _____

3. Go play somewhere else. We don't want you on our team.
   _____
   _____

4. Why don't you get some new clothes? Nobody wears **that** anymore!
   _____
   _____

5. Nobody wants to play with **you**, Monkey-Face!
   _____
   _____

6. Ha! You got the lowest grade in the class on the science test! Dummy!
   _____
   _____

7. Hey, Dog-Breath! Did someone steal your toothbrush?
   _____
   _____

POSTER

SUPPLEMENTARY ACTIVITY #1

I'm an O.K. Kid!

Objective   Students will realize that internalizing put-downs diminishes self-esteem.

Materials   One piece of 11" x 17" paper with the words "I'm an O.K. Kid" written on it in large letters

Supplementary Activity #1 Transparency/Handout, "I'm an O.K. Kid"

Procedure   Tell students that you are going to tell them a story that will demonstrate how hard it is for people to respect themselves if they believe the put-downs they receive. Proceed by telling them the following story:

It was Lucy's first day at her new school. She was a little worried about what might happen, but her parents reminded her that she was well liked in her old school and had lots of friends there. They told her that she was such a neat kid that she would make new friends in no time. Lucy believed what her parents said because it was true. She did have a lot of friends. So, she went to her new school thinking, "I'm an O.K. kid." *Hold up the 11" x 17" paper with those words written on it.*

Lucy began her first day by going with the rest of her class to the nurse's office, where the nurse weighed and measured each student. When Lucy's turn came, she stepped on the scale to be weighed and measured. Lucy always knew that she was taller than most of the kids her age. What she had not realized was that because of her height, she also weighed more than most other kids her age. As the nurse called out her weight to be written down by an assistant, Lucy heard someone in her class say, "Boy is that new kid FAT! She weighs ten pounds more than anyone else in our class. Talk about a Lardo!"

Soon after, several kids began calling her "Lardo Lucy." She thought to herself, "Gee, I must be too fat." She didn't think she was such an O.K. kid anymore. In fact, her O.K. feeling went from this size *(hold up the paper with the words "I'm an O.K. Kid")* **to about this size** *(fold paper in half)*. **Along with her O.K. feeling went a lot of her courage to go up to kids she didn't know and talk to them. She began to act quiet**

and shy instead of showing how friendly and fun she was. The other kids didn't really see what she was like. Since they didn't know her, even more kids started calling her "Lardo Lucy." As her nickname spread, her O.K. feeling got even smaller. *Fold paper in half again.*

Later that day the teacher gave everyone a math test. Lucy had been pretty good in math in her old school, but in her new school the teacher was using a different book and the students were doing things Lucy had never been taught to do. When she got her paper back, she saw that she had gotten almost all the problems wrong. The boy next to her noticed it, too, and said in a loud voice, "You got 29 wrong!" Another kid said to her, "Boy, you're a real math whiz!" The O.K. feeling that Lucy had left got even smaller. *Fold paper in half again.* Lucy told herself that she was dumb and fat. Every time she said this to herself, she felt less O.K. *Make another fold in the paper.*

At recess nobody invited Lucy to play, and when she walked toward a group of kids, they walked away. She said to herself, "Nobody likes me at this school." Being ignored by the kids hurt even more than anything else that had happened that day, and her good feeling about herself got even smaller. *Fold the paper once again.*

The final straw for Lucy occurred during P.E. The kids were taking turns walking on the balance beam. When it was Lucy's turn, she got up on the beam and was just starting to take a step when some kid shouted out, "Don't let Lardo Lucy on the beam. She'll snap it in two!" At that moment, Lucy lost her balance. She heard somebody mumble, "Klutz!" and she told herself that she was too fat and clumsy to make it even a few steps on the balance beam. *Fold the paper another time.* Her self-respect got even smaller. She walked sadly to the end of the line. Because she believed the put-downs she was given and didn't challenge them in her mind, this is about all she had left of that wonderful O.K. feeling she'd come to her new school with that morning. *Hold up the paper, now folded into a tiny piece.*

It looks like Lucy needs somebody to help her not let put-downs get to her and to teach her not to repeat them to herself and believe them. Let's go back through Lucy's day at her new school and see if we can help her get back the O.K. feeling she used to have. *Show*

Supplementary Activity #1 Transparency, "I'm an O.K. Kid." **This is a list of some encouraging self-statements that would help Lucy keep her self-esteem from shrinking.**

Which of these statements could Lucy have used when she fell off the balance beam? *Invite student response. Then unfold the 11" x 17" paper once.* **Right. If she had encouraged herself in this way, her self-esteem would at least have been this size.**

What could she have said to herself when the students walked away from her at recess? *After students respond, unfold the paper once more.* **If Lucy had said these things to herself, her self-esteem would have been this size.**

What could Lucy have said to herself instead of telling herself she was dumb and fat? *Unfold the paper again.*

What could she have said to herself when the kids gave her a hard time about getting so many problems wrong on her math test? *Unfold the paper yet another time.* **Wow, her positive feelings about herself sure are growing again!**

What could Lucy have said to herself when more kids gave her the nickname "Lardo Lucy"? *Unfold the paper again.* **Notice how her self-esteem is getting bigger and bigger as she uses positive self-talk instead of listening to and believing the put-downs she is given.**

Finally, what could Lucy have said to herself when she first heard the kids say that she was fat? *Unfold the paper to its original size.* **Right! Now Lucy's got that wonderful O.K. feeling about herself back because she hasn't let the put-downs get to her by believing them or by repeating them to herself.**

SUPPLEMENTARY ACTIVITY #1 TRANSPARENCY/HANDOUT

"I'm an O.K. Kid!"

- I'm not going to let a few people's comments make me think I don't look right.

- I'm tall, not fat, and being tall has lots of advantages.

- I don't like what they are saying but I can live with it.

- I'll find the right friends for me someday.

- This hurts my feelings, but I won't die because of it.

- Things are always changing. This will, too.

- They don't know what I'm really like.

- Someone must have hurt his feelings a lot and he's taking his hurt out on me.

- No matter what they say, I know I'm O.K.

- When they get to know me, they'll like me.

- They're just trying to act cool.

- So I made a mistake. I'm not a professional.

- I won't give up. I will get someone to show me how to do this.

- Other people like me.

- I can do this if I stick with it.

- There are other things that I do really well in school.

SUPPLEMENTARY ACTIVITY #2

Shielding Yourself From Put-Downs

You can shield yourself from put-downs by saying kind things to yourself. On the lines below, write some helpful self-statements you could make to shield yourself when someone puts you down.

SUPPLEMENTARY ACTIVITY #3

Keeping Count

Objective   Students will become aware of positive and negative interactions in their classroom by keeping a tally of put-downs and friendly comments they overhear during a three-week period.

Materials   Supplementary Activity #3 Handout/Transparency, "Keeping Count" (one handout per student)

Procedure   Tell students you need their help in making their classroom a warmer, friendlier place. Explain that one way they can help is to keep a record of all the put-downs and friendly comments they hear in the classroom. Give them each a "Keeping Count" tally sheet (Supplementary Activity #3 Handout) and tell them that they are to keep it on their desks every day for the next three weeks, making a mark to indicate every put-down or friendly comment they hear. At the end of each day, take an average of their counts and write the totals on the transparency that matches the student handout. Talk with the class about the number of put-downs and friendly comments recorded for that day. Compare the results at the end of each week. Have the students continue to keep this tally for three weeks to track any improvement in the ratio of negative to positive comments. Surprise them with a reward, such as an extra art period, free-choice time, or an extra recess, if they show an increase in friendly comments and a decrease in put-downs over the three-week period.

VARIATION 1

You may wish to have two or three students, rather than the whole class, keep the tally each day. Be sure that every student who's interested has an opportunity to be a Tally Kid during the three-week period.

VARIATION 2

You may wish to enlarge the tally sheet to poster size and put it up in the classroom. Then you could have students mark the class poster instead of individual tally sheets when they hear put-downs or friendly comments. To minimize class disruption, allow them to go to the poster only at selected times during the day.

Put-Downs   Friendly Comments

SUPPLEMENTARY ACTIVITY #3 HANDOUT/TRANSPARENCY

Keeping Count

	😠 PUT-DOWNS	☀ KIND COMMENTS
Monday		
Tuesday		
Wednesday		
Thursday		
Friday		

1

	😠 PUT-DOWNS	☀ KIND COMMENTS
Monday		
Tuesday		
Wednesday		
Thursday		
Friday		

2

	😠 PUT-DOWNS	☀ KIND COMMENTS
Monday		
Tuesday		
Wednesday		
Thursday		
Friday		

3

SUPPLEMENTARY ACTIVITY #4

What to Do If an Adult Puts You Down

Objective Students will learn appropriate responses to put-downs given by adults and will brainstorm ways to encourage themselves with positive self-talk.

Materials Supplementary Activity #3 Transparency - "What to Do If an Adult Puts You Down"

Procedure Tell students that today they'll be talking about what to do if an adult says something to them that is a put-down. Explain to students that adults won't accept put-downs back from children. Adults also won't accept a joking response, or an agreeing remark that doesn't sound sincere. The wisest response for a child is usually to remain silent and do what he or she is told.

Tell students that there **may** be times, however, when they can respond to the adult without being rude. If they feel they need to respond, saying one or another of these statements (or a variation on them) will usually be effective:

- "I'm sorry."

- "I'm trying to do better."

- "I feel bad when you say things like that."

Explain to students that whether or not they feel they need to make a response, they can **always** help themselves feel better when they've been put down by telling themselves an encouraging self-statement. Three encouraging things they might say are:

- "I'm not bad, I'm young."

- "My behavior isn't always good, but **I'm** good."

- "Little by little, I **am** improving."

Show students the transparency, "What to Do If an Adult Puts You Down." Use the scenarios following, which fit the pictures. Alternate asking students to say which statement they think would be good to say or to think to themselves. For each statement, have students put their thumbs up if they think that it would be a good idea to use that statement. To assist them in understanding how to fit a response to a situation, it may be helpful to comment on why a particular statement might be appropriate or inappropriate.

You may wish to extend this learning by teaching Lesson 14, "What To Do When an Adult Is Angry at You," in the ASSIST manual *Helping Kids Handle Anger.*

Use the following scenarios or make up ones of your own:

- This woman is the boy's neighbor. She's yelling at him for leaving her gate open, because it let her dog out of the yard. She's saying that he's "brainless" and "can't be trusted to do anything right."

- This man is angry because the girl accidentally knocked over a stack of trays in his restaurant. He says, "You're so clumsy it's amazing that you could even cross the street to get here!"

- This boy has been playing with his friend outside the woman's window and making a lot of noise. She says, "You noisy brat—you don't have any consideration for other people!"

- This man says to the girl, "Boy, are you ever doing a crummy job playing that video game! Why don't you just give up!"

- This boy chained his bike to the woman's fence. The woman says, "Who said you could do that? You're just a troublemaker, aren't you?"

- This man is angry and is telling the girl that she's a "spoiled brat" because she didn't wait her turn in line at the check-out stand.

SUPPLEMENTARY ACTIVITY #4 TRANSPARENCY

What to Do If an Adult Puts You Down

You can say something like . . .

1. "I understand why you feel that way. I'm trying to do better."

2. "I feel bad when you say things like that."

3. "It hurts my feelings when you say that."

4. _____

5. _____

You can think something like . . .

1. "My behavior isn't always good, but I'm good."

2. "I'm not bad; I'm just young."

3. "Little by little, I'm improving."

4. _____

5. _____

An Imaginary Letter to Someone You Tease

Objective   Students will think about whether they may be teasing someone for differences that can't be changed and will write an imaginary letter to that person.

Materials   Supplementary Activity #5 Handout, "An Imaginary Letter to Someone You Tease"

Procedure   Talk to students about the fact that there are always some people we like a lot, some we like a little, and a few we don't like at all. Ask them to think of someone they don't like. Then ask them to answer the following questions, either in their minds or on scratch paper:

- What is it you don't like about that person?

- Is the person different from you?

- How is he or she different from you?

- Do you ever tease the person because of these differences?

- Can the person change these differences?

- How do you think the person feels about these differences?

- Can you let it be O.K. for the person to be different from you?

Next, instruct the students to write an imaginary letter to that person they tease. At the end of the letter they'll have an opportunity to tell the person that they're going to try to stop teasing him or her about their differences. Distribute copies of Supplementary Activity #4 Handout, "An Imaginary Letter to Someone You Tease." (You may wish to make a transparency of it and use the transparency to guide the class through the activity.) Either collect the letters or have students take them home to assure anonymity.

SUPPLEMENTARY ACTIVITY #5 HANDOUT

An Imaginary Letter to Someone You Tease

Dear _____:

I tease you because _____

_____

_____

 I wish you would change _____

_____

_____

I know you can't change _____

_____

_____

You and I are different. Sometimes it's hard for me to be nice to people who are different from me. I know differences are O.K., though.

I'll try to stop teasing you about _____.

Signed,

Me

POSTER

Don't give put-downs.